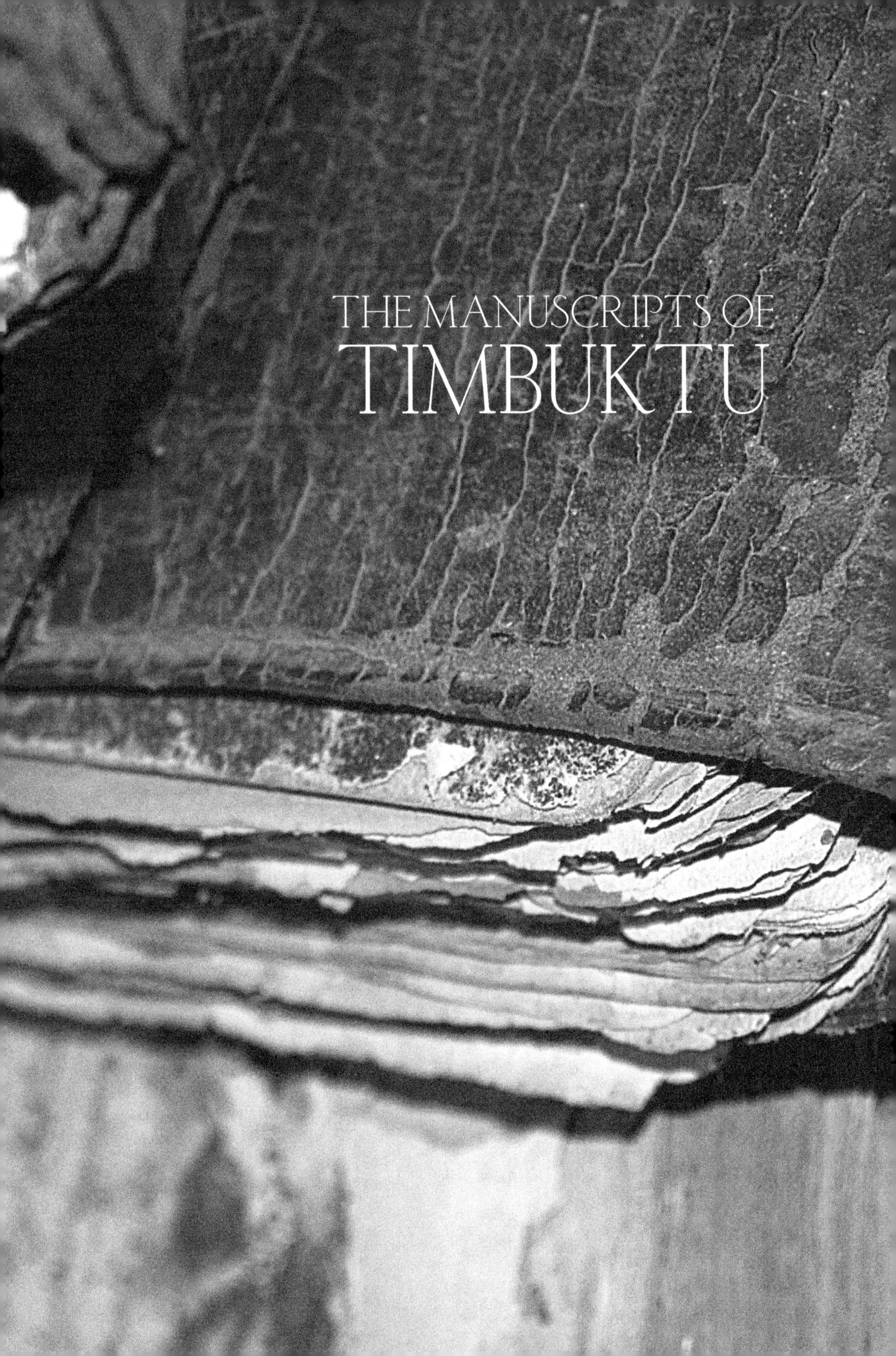

THE MANUSCRIPTS OF TIMBUKTU

THE MANUSCRIPTS OF TIMBUKTU

Jean-Michel Djian

Translated by Christopher Wise

Preface by J.M.G. Le Clézio

Afterword by Souleyman Bachir Diagne

AFRICA WORLD PRESS
TRENTON | LONDON | CAPE TOWN | NAIROBI | ADDIS ABABA | ASMARA | IBADAN | NEW DELHI

AFRICA WORLD PRESS
541 West Ingham Avenue | Suite B
Trenton, New Jersey 08638

First French Edition: 2012
First AWP English Edition: 2020

Library of Congress Cataloging-in-Publication Data

Names: Djian, Jean-Michel, author. | Wise, Christopher, 1961- translator. | Le Clâezio, J.-M. G. (Jean-Marie Gustave), 1940- writer of foreword. | Diagne, Souleymane Bachir, writer of afterword.
Title: The manuscripts of Timbuktu : secrets, myths, and realities / Jean-Michel Djian ; translated by Christopher Wise ; preface by J.M.G. Le Clezio ; afterword by Souleyman Bachir Diagne.
Other titles: Manuscrits de Tombouctou. English
Description: Trenton, New Jersey : Africa World Press, 2019. | "First French Edition 2012."
Identifiers: LCCN 2019005909 | ISBN 9781569026380 (pb)
Subjects: LCSH: Manuscripts, Arabic--Mali--Tombouctou. | Tombouctou (Mali)--History.
Classification: LCC Z6620.M42 D5513 2019 | DDC 091.096623--dc23
LC record available at https://lccn.loc.gov/2019005909

My writing is really orality
captured on paper.

AMADOU HAMPÂTÉ BÂ

[NOTE: All page numbers refer to the published
French version of the text.]

With Contributions From:

Georges Bohas, Professor of Arabic at ENS Lyon, founder of the VECMAS Program (Development, Editing, and Criticism of Sub-Saharan Manuscripts in Arabic).

Cheikh Hamidou Kane, writer, author of *Ambiguous Adventure*, a classic of African literature.

Doulaye Konate, Doctor of History and Archeology, Department Chair of the École Normale Supérieure at the University of Mali in Bamako, President of the National Association of Malian Historians.

Mahmoud Zouber, Historian, Inaugural Director of the Ahmed-Baba Center of Timbuktu, now the Ahmed-Baba Institute of Advanced Studies and Islamic Research.

And with the extremely valuable collaboration of the photographer **Seydou Camara d'Abdel Kader Haidara**, Director of the Mamma-Haidara Library, and of the following scholars: **Saad Traore**, **Floréal Sanagustin**, and **Mohammed Hamady**.

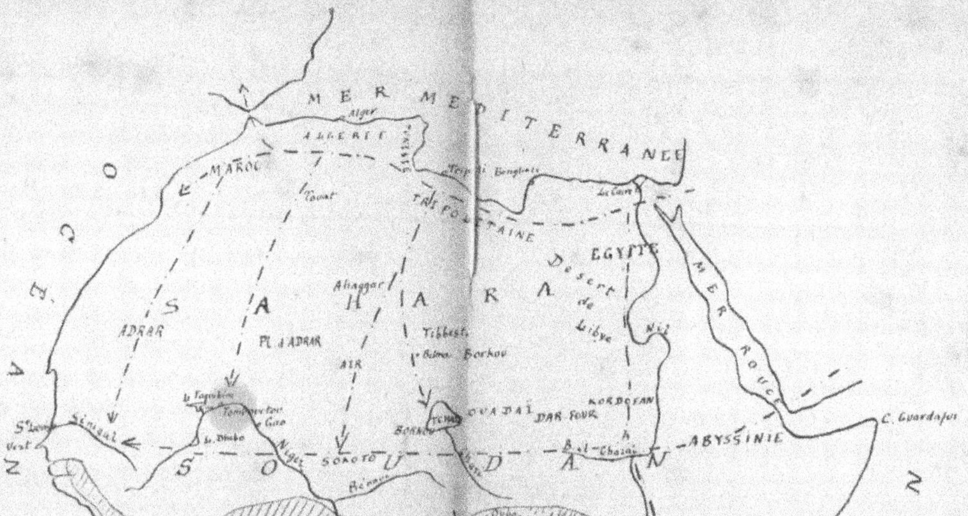

MER MEDITERRANEE
Alger
ALGERIE
TUNISIE
MAROC
Tripoli
Benghasi
Le Caire
TRIPOLITAINE
EGYPTE
Désert de Libye
MER ROUGE
OCÉAN ATLANTIQUE
SAHARA
ADRAR
Pl. d'ADRAR
Ahaggar
AIR
Tibbest
Borkou
TCHAD
OUADAÏ
DAR FOUR
KORDOFAN
ABYSSINIE
C. Guardafui
Nil
St Louis
Vert
Sénégal
Tombouctou
Gao
Niger
SOKOTO
BORNOU
Bénoué
SOUDAN
Côte de l'Ivoire
Golfe de Guinée
Oubangui
Congo
L. Albert
L. Victoria Nyanza
Mt Kenia
Mt Kilima Njaro
L. Tanganyika
L. Nyassa
Zambèze
OCÉAN INDIEN
ANGOLA
Désert de Kalahari
RHODESIA
TRANSVAAL
Vaal
ORANGE
Orange
COL. du CAP
Le Cap
C. de Bonne Espérance
Légende
Voies historiques des migrations de peuples
La grande forêt

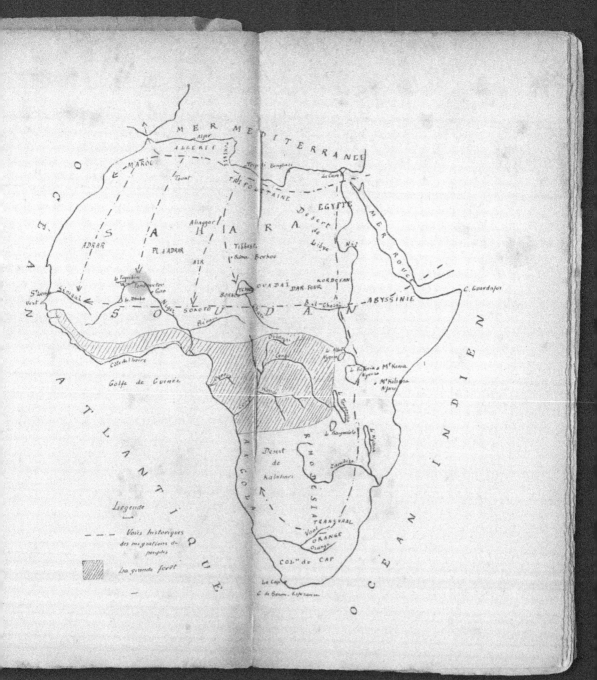

Editor's Note

Early in the summer, just as we completed preparation of this book, the General Director of UNESCO, Ms. Irinka Bokova called upon the nations that border Mali "to do everything in their power to prevent the destruction and trafficking of ancient manuscripts," as reported during Spring 2012 in the vicinity of Timbuktu.

Armed rebels who had taken control of northern Mali openly encouraged the theft and destruction of ancient documents despite the fact that for nearly two decades the international community had called for the development and preservation of this exceptional written heritage from the Sahel, especially in Timbuktu.

Our hope is that this new work from Jean-Michel Djian will enable the reader to appreciate the seriousness of this new development. But we also hope that this book may signal a renewed awareness of the rich culture of the Sahel.

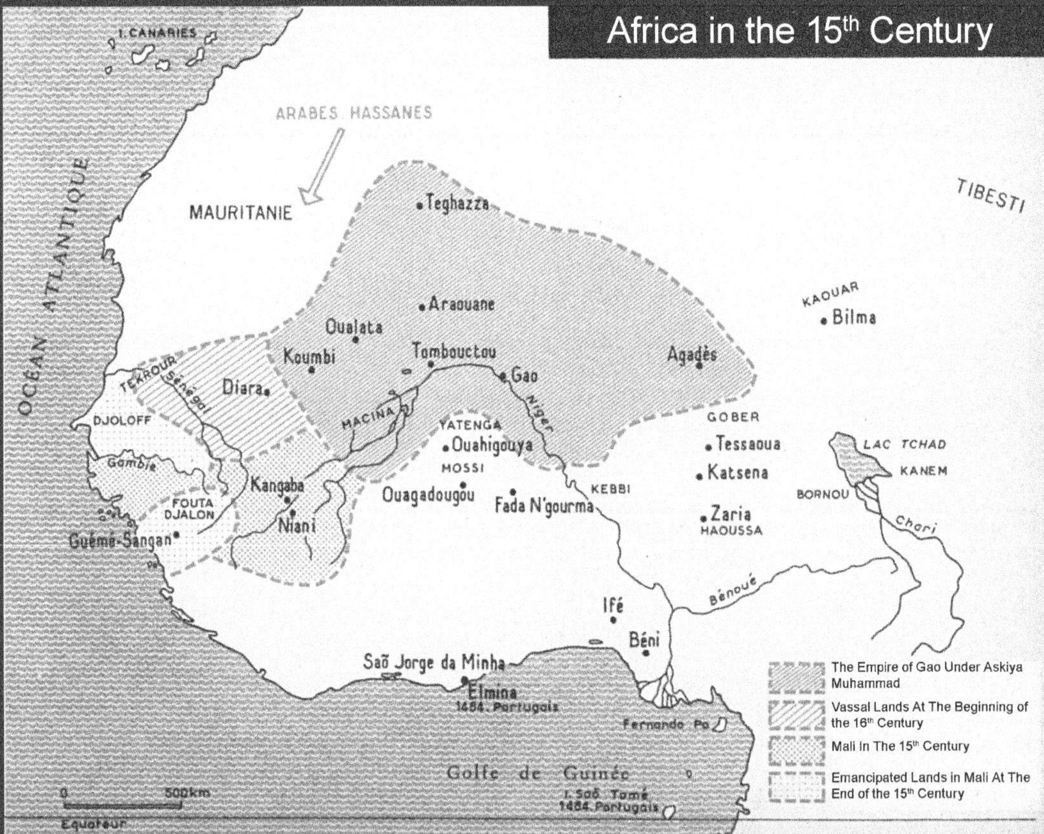
Africa in the 15th Century
I. CANARIES
ARABES HASSANES
OCÉAN ATLANTIQUE
MAURITANIE
TIBESTI
Teghazza
Araouane
Oualata
Koumbi
Tombouctou
Gao
Agadès
KAOUAR
Bilma
TEKROUR
Sénégal
Diara
DJOLOFF
Gambie
MACINA
Niger
YATENGA
Ouahigouya
MOSSI
Ouagadougou
Fada N'gourma
Kangaba
Niani
FOUTA DJALON
Guémé-Sangan
KEBBI
GOBER
Tessaoua
Katsena
Zaria
HAOUSSA
LAC TCHAD
KANEM
BORNOU
Chari
Bénoué
Ifé
Béni
São Jorge da Minha
Elmina
1484. Portugais
Fernando Po
Golfe de Guinée
I. São Tomé
1484. Portugais
0 500km
Equateur
The Empire of Gao Under Askiya Muhammad
Vassal Lands At The Beginning of the 16th Century
Mali In The 15th Century
Emancipated Lands in Mali At The End of the 15th Century

Table of Contents

Commentary on a grammatical poem (216 verses) written by Hazim Al Qartajanni (1211-1285).

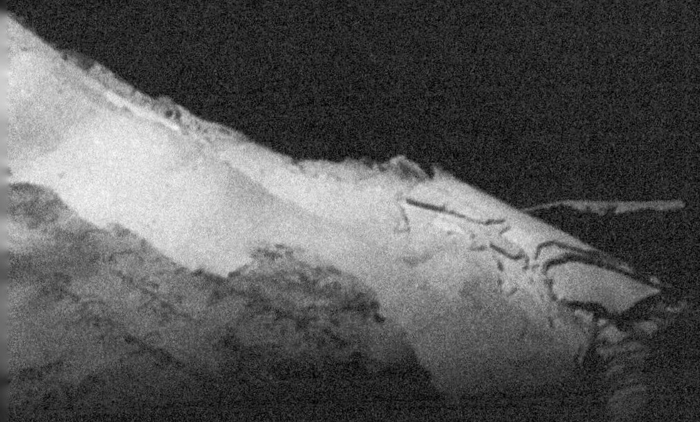

Translator's Preface

by Christopher Wise

The appearance of Jean-Michel Djian's *The Manuscripts of Timbuktu: Secrets, Myths, and Realities* is an event worthy of celebration. Seydou Camara's stunning photographs, Djian's own thoughtful contributions, brief essays from various scholars in the field, and translated excerpts from the manuscripts themselves make this the best place to start for anyone interested in Timbuktu and its written heritage. General readers and specialists alike will be pleased with what they find here.

Djian addresses the historical neglect of the Timbuktu manuscripts in the European context (and, by extension, the global community). For the Anglophone world, the neglect of these manuscripts is perhaps even more scandalous than in the Francophone world. Although the Songhay *Tarikhs* have been available in French for more than a hundred years, they have only recently appeared in English: Al Sa'di's *Tarikh al-sudan* was published in 1999 and Al Hajj Mahmud Kati's *Tarikh al-fattash* was published in 2011. This raises the obvious question, "Why did it take so long for these important documents to appear in English?"

There are at least three answers to this question. First, they did not appear in English because of racism against black people. The fact that they have only recently appeared, and that they remain largely unknown, is due to racial prejudice, especially in U.S. institutions of higher learning. Second, there has not been as much interest in the English-speaking world in these manuscripts because French-speaking peoples colonized the Sahel, not English-speaking peoples. Colonial and neo-colonial powers with their many vested interests tend to take a hands-off approach to the spoils of their neighbors. *Noblesse oblige.* Third, the fault lies at the door of the scholarly pedant and his fear of books that are written in his field for the general reader. This type of academic does not want the knowledge he possesses to circulate too widely from fear that he may become irrelevant. In fact, his fears are justified, for pedantry is the guise of scholarly mediocrity.

Djian and the many other contributors to this important new book certainly do not belong to the latter category. They have done a praiseworthy job in taking an extraordinarily complex phenomenon and making it accessible to all who may be interested. They are to be congratulated, for the information that this book contains certainly deserves the widest possible dissemination. In fact, these scholars document a discovery that is no less important than the French discovery of the Rosetta Stone in 1799 (the same year that Mungo Park's *Travels* appeared).

Prior to the appearance of recent English-language translations of the *Tarikhs*, and now Djian's important new volume, wider knowledge of these texts in the Anglophone world first came via Ralph Manheim's translation of Yambo Ouologuem's *Bound To Violence*, (recently retranslated as *The Duty of Violence*). In the late 1960s, Ouologuem wrote a brilliant and award-winning novel that was also a parody of the *Tarikhs*. But what exactly *were* the "*Tarikhs*," many wondered? It was not until Thomas Hale wrote *Scribe, Griot, Novelist* (1990) that a book-length discussion of the Songhay chronicles would appear in English (some nine years before the first *Tarikh* was translated into English). Hale compared the *Tarikhs* to the Songhay griot epic and Ouologuem's novel. He also drew upon the valuable research of the renowned scholar of Timbuktu manuscripts, John Hunwick. Now, both the major Songhay *Tarikhs* (or "chronicles") are available in English, and readers can investigate their relative merits for themselves.

What remains to be said is that *The Duty of Violence* was first and foremost a critique of Arab imperialism in West Africa. Like Ouologuem, Djian does not dodge this controversial question. In the aftermath of recent events in Mali, the fall of Gao and Timbuktu to Wahhabi extremists, this question has perhaps never been more urgent. In the *Tarikh al fattash*, descriptions of the Sa'adian (Moroccan) destruction of the Songhay Empire of the Askiyas at the end of the 16th century may seem oddly contemporary when compared with recent journalistic descriptions of jihadi acts in "Azawad." Those who hope to make sense of what is happening in Mali today could do no better than start with a carefully reading of the *Tarikhs*.

Yesterday and today, invaders from the north who imagined that the Sahel uniquely belonged to them as blood descendants of the Prophet Muhammad sacked and looted an ancient black African civilization. When the Ansar Dine took control of Timbuktu in 2013, they not only destroyed many of Timbuktu's manuscripts, they also smashed the tombs of its saints and destroyed many other artifacts that they deemed heretical. The truth is that the Ansar Dine, AQIM, and other jihadis were right to fear Timbuktu's ancient manuscripts. This is so because the information that they contain shows that the interpretation of Islam developed by the Songhay people was an *African* one. These manuscripts have little to offer racist Muslims like the Ansar Dine (or any other Arabist or Wahhabist militant group).

As Dijan documents, Timbuktu's manuscripts are filled with information about local customs and inscriptions practices that emanate from what Hale and

Paul Stoller have called its "deep Sahelian matrix." These practices include oath-swearing on the tombs of saints; the writing of magical amulets, as well as charms and squares; the drinking of Quranic surahs; cursing; soothsaying; conjuration, and so on. The culture from which these practices emerge is older than the Islamic religion, older than all the Abrahamic religions.

It is important to remember then that the manuscripts that are so beautifully photographed here are not manuscripts that were written by Arab Muslims, but by black Muslims who successfully Africanized Islam. It is not the case then that these texts were written by black Africans who had undergone Arabization after coming into contact with white peoples from the north. The manuscripts of Timbuktu are underwritten by authentically Sahelian views of the world that have nothing to do with dogmatic and Arabist varieties of Islam that today inspire the militants of ISIS and Al Qaeda. These manuscripts stand as powerful witnesses against Wahhabist and sharifan ideologues. They also help us to understand that imperial ventures in West Africa from the north have never been about the Islamic religion, but imperial conquest.

Despite the debacle of Azawad, it is exciting to reflect upon the discoveries about Africa that lie before us, thanks to these manuscripts. Djian and other contributors to this volume have done an outstanding job of communicating that growing sense of excitement among scholars today.

Bellingham, 2016

Further reading:

Thomas A. Hale and Nouhou Malio, *The Epic of Askia Mohammed* (Bloomington and Indianapolis: Indiana University Press, 1996).

Christopher Wise (ed.), *The Yambo Ouologuem Reader: The Duty of Violence, A Black Ghostwriter's Letter to France* (Trenton, New Jersey: Africa World Press, 2009).

Thomas A. Hale, *Scribe, Griot, Novelist: Narrative Interpreters of the Songhay Empire* (Gainesville: University Presses of Florida, 1990).

John Hunwick, *Timbuktu & the Songhay Empire: Al-Sa'di's Tarikh al-sudan down to 1613 & other Contemporary Documents* (Leiden: Brill, 1999).

Christopher Wise (ed.) *The Timbuktu Chronicles, 1493-1599: Al Hajj Mahmud Kati's Tarikh al-fattash* (Trenton, New Jersey: Africa World Press, 2011).

Timbuktu, Words Into Gold

J.M.G. Le Clézio

The name itself reverberates across two centuries. In France, England, and Germany, the tales of early travelers who ventured into the desert -- Barth, Mungo Park, Camille Douls, and René Caillié – nurtured this marvelous and notorious legend. Its very name stirred up fantasies of gold from Mali's and Songhay's lost empires, enough gold to destabilize the entire market, the mirage of caravans and giant pirogues navigating a great river, not yet called the Niger, a river whose origin and sources remained unknown. The mysterious city of Timbuktu, a forbidden city for Christians, the key to the north and the land of the blacks in the desert, Assouad, the Sudan, a boundless immensity. Did they know it? These French and German adventurers, Barth, Laing, but most of all Caillié, the humble peasant and son of a galley slave? Did they realize that they did not walk the footpaths of barbarians but ventured into the land of the book? How could they have known? For these men, portents of colonial conquest, the interior of Africa was not the black continent but a crucible of diverse races. It was a wild and mysterious frontier. But it was also a land of unfathomable riches. If they called it "wild," they did so in order to tame it. For the world they entered was the last latch upon a door that had long been closed to Christian civilization.

What kind of land had they ventured into? Timbuktu was the object of their desire. It fixed the limit of the North African desert and the immense savannahs and forests that blanketed Benin's southern coasts. Timbuktu was the first great fort on the river. Situated between "Moorish" lands (Morocco, the Western Sahara, Algeria, Mali), it was the final destination along the caravan routes. It was situated at the far edge of the land of the Tuareg camel riders in their vast desert kingdom: to the East lay the lands of the Fulani and Hausa, and to the South the Mande grasslands. The caravan route was the royal road to the world of the desert: It linked the oases of Walata and Chinguetti in Adrar as far south as the great and holy city of Jenne and as far north as Smara. René Caillié, one of the first travelers to Timbuktu (after Laing who was killed there), entered the town disguised as a poor itinerant merchant. After a long adventure on foot, Caillié's dreams of gold and other marvels came to an abrupt end. Upon first glimpse, he said, Timbuktu seemed little more than "a mass of mud houses, badly constructed. In every direction, there were immense plains of shifting sand, a whiteness that was tinged with yellow, and the greatest aridity. The sky along the horizon was pale red. Nature itself seemed sad, and the greatest silence imaginable reigned in this place. Not a single bird could be heard singing. " And yet, he added, "there was something imposing in the sight of a great town that was built in the midst of so much sand. You could not help but admire the efforts of those who had founded it." The traveler did not find the great wealth that he had hoped to find. Timbuktu's ruler Shaykh Usman in no way resembled the sultans from the thousand and one nights: "Nothing distinguishes him from anyone else in this town," Caillié noted. "He dresses like the Moors of Morocco. There is no more luxury in his house than in those of the Moorish merchants." On the other hand, Shaykh Usman seemed to the young peasant from Saintonge to be a man possessing all the traits of the enlightened monarch, a mythical figure during the French revolution of 1789. "The King does not receive any tribute from his people nor from foreign merchants; but, he does accept gifts," Caillié wrote. "He is not really the head of an administration: he is more like the father of a large family who governs his children. He is just and good and has nothing to fear from his subjects. His gentle and simple manners are undoubtedly akin to those of the Biblical patriarchs." At a second glance, Timbuktu seemed to this young Frenchman to be a model society. Despite the personal risks he ran there, it seemed to him a peaceful and harmonious place. Even the practice of slavery in Timbuktu seemed relatively more humane. He noted that the slaves of the Sudan, after they were sold to merchants from the north, shed a great many tears when they were forced to leave this town. In fact, between the cruelty of the Tuaregs, who pillaged and robbed travelers in the north, and the violence of the Mande in the south, Timbuktu seemed a tranquil and comfortable oasis of peace. But Caillié had little to say about the writing culture of this village. His disguise as a poor traveling merchant did not permit him access to its libraries – in particular, to the library of Prince

Usman. But he noted that, "All the blacks of Timbuktu are able to read the Quran. They even learn it by heart. Children are required to learn it at an early age. This is the case whether their parents oversee their education themselves or entrust it to the Moors, whom they deem to be the most highly educated. They also communicate with Jenne through the use of writing."

This sandy and extraordinarily hot land, where the only thing that grows is the thorn bush, also happens to be the land of the written word. In Timbuktu, the written word enters into the city along two separate paths: the first descends from the north and follows a chain of desert oases, a long chain of holy towns connecting Timbuktu and Jenne to the Maghreb and Libya. The second, less well-known but no less important, nourishes the cultures in the south, the Futa Jalon, Ghana, the heirs to the ancient empires of Mali, Songhay, or Nigeria. This region is also the land of the Foumban hieroglyphs from Cameron, the Igbo petroglyphs, and the Tamashek writings of the desert.

It would be foolish and absurd to oppose the oral word to the written word in African history. Due to our growing awareness of the desert libraries of the Adrar, especially in Walata and Chinguetti, not to mention the vast libraries of Timbuktu, our understanding of the cultural complexity of this so-called "illiterate" world has significantly evolved. Jean-Michel Djian's attractive new book too makes an important contribution to our growing understanding of this complex history.

But if we really want to make sense of a discovery of such magnitude, we must dare to embark upon a voyage of exploration that René Caillié never imagined. The destination of this journey is a vast culture that sits on the desert's doorstep, a land that has long played its part in history, but that has also been subject to pillage and conquest.

To begin, let's be frank about what has impeded recognition of this desert culture. The biggest factor has been colonization. The various colonial powers' theft of Central Africa, each in their own way, plunged the region into a state of shock. One consequence was the loss of memory. Writing is fragile by its very nature. Its main nemesis is not humidity, decay, or even oblivion, but human violence. The French, Spanish, and British troops that finally penetrated a land once protected by the hostility of its climate, as well as the ferocity of its nomadic tribes, were hardly interested in exploring the region's cultural hubs and libraries. At Smara,

Adar, and Chinguetti, military assaults and fires destroyed a large part of this cultural memory, while the ignorance of the foreign soldiers did the rest. Senghor evokes the image of precious manuscripts that were lit up as torches. It is not difficult to imagine how wind, looting, and neglect must have played a role in their destruction. But colonial violence itself is insufficient to account for everything. The economic catastrophe that devastated the continent at the beginning of the modern era also indirectly bears responsibility for the cultural invisibility of these manuscripts. The fall of the great empires like Mali or Bornou, Europe's penetration into Ashanti lands and Benin, the sale of firearms, and, above all, the global slave trade, destroyed the equilibrium that had once existed between nations, sometimes upsetting social structures and the old order, particularly in places where knowledge and the arts played an important role. In the more remote regions, where hunger never ceases to gnaw at the human spirit, the preservation of ancient culture could hardly have been a top priority for those who were struggling to survive. And yet, the manuscripts of Timbuktu *have* miraculously survived, most of them locked up in family vaults or hidden in the local madrasas. Today, they offer Africa's indigenous peoples a real chance to insure the survival of their ancient culture into the future. They stand guard over African culture in a land now gripped by upheaval.

Earlier, I referred to the power of the spoken word. Without this power, writing could not exist. The manuscripts that are held in Timbuktu, like those described and photographed here, reveal the intimate relation between the spoken and written word. In their vast scope, these texts are also bound to the nomadic culture of the desert, its history, the poetry of the oasis bards, and the scholarly traditions of the great religious centers. In fact, they are the product of the African imagination. While many of these manuscripts are commentaries on the Quran and the Hadith, there are also animal fables, epic narratives, poems in rhyme (the Qasida in *ra*, for example), proverbs, even advice on sexual and medicinal remedies. Those who investigate this literature will also find treatises on astronomy, geography, and mathematics, for these sciences too were the passion of the desert people. The libraries of the great religious leaders like the 15th century saint Ahmad Al Aroussi or Shaykh Ma Al Ainine of the Western Sahara, as well as those from the modern era, clearly attest to these facts. Many of these libraries have disappeared, their archives cast to the winds after years of looting and pillage. Only the most patient of researchers today will be able to solve the many mysteries that they pose to us, the barely legible residue of an ancient civilization.

For, the importance of these manuscripts has little to do with nostalgia or some remotely exotic and esoteric knowledge. These rediscovered texts are both humble and magnificent in appearance. Sometimes they are richly ornamented and bound. But, whatever their outward condition, they stand today as a witness to the inherent injustice of our universal culture. An important part of the world's civilization remains faceless. In opposition to the *idées récues* passed down to us from the European travelers of the 19th century, but also tourist companies in our own day, these immense Saharan territories have never been depopulated lands. This vast swath of earth that divides the two Africa's, and that resembles a lunar landscape, was never a border between the civilized and literate north and the primitive and obscure south. Timbuktu was a critical juncture for Sub-Saharan Africa. Its religious, philosophical, and scientific thought was as highly evolved as the many texts based that are upon it, including those that address issues of law, politics, and wisdom. The core of this thought drew upon fables as well as history. Both revealed the broad linguistic scope of African thought, its mixed heritages, including tales of Persian if not Indian origin (*The History of Hassan Al Basari*), Hebraic origin (*The History of Buluqya*), Biblical accounts, early writings from the era of Islam's birth, as well as tales and poems in the Hassaniya language (a local language closely related to Yemenite Arabic that is spoken from Laayun to southern Morocco and as far into the Sahara as Timbuktu.) The painful situation now besetting this region, including the possibility that Timbuktu's manuscripts could be destroyed, reveals just how urgent it is that we now begin to recognize and protect this universal human inheritance. Jean-Michel Djian's marvelous book invites us to reconsider our long-standing errors in judgment about the region's history. It also encourages us to be more humble in the future, even as it inspires us to do all that we can today to rescue Africa's libraries.

Udo, May 2012

Introduction

For nearly a thousand years, the Sahel's most enigmatic city has tantalized the outside world, sometimes with its commerce in salt and gold, sometimes with its intellectual heritage and flamboyant architecture. Merely to travel to this Malian city with a population of some thirty thousand, about a thousand miles north of Bamako, has been the dream of countless curious travelers, pilgrims, and explorers. All imagined that they were embarking upon an epic adventure of mythical proportions.

René Caillé stayed in Timbuktu for thirty days in 1828. The anthropologist Heinrich Barth was the next to arrive in 1853 (see the accounts of René Caillié, Heinrich Barth, and Félix Dubois, p. 32). The German scientist Barth was one of the first Europeans to discover the manuscripts of the city, in particular, the *Tarikh al-sudan* by Abderrahmane Al Sa'di. This chronicle described the social life of West African peoples in the 17th century. Far more than its gold or salt, Timbuktu's manuscripts have always been its real treasure.

At the heart of Sub-Saharan Africa during the 15th and 16th centuries, the flourishing city of Timbuktu attracted teachers and students. Both enjoyed the protection of the Songhay Emperor, most notably the Askiya Muhammad. From this great site of learning, knowledge was widely shared and disseminated. Teaching and books fared well in Timbuktu, as did the professions that profited from its learning: copyists, bookstores, tutors, bookbinders, translators, illuminators...

Some students came from as far as Egypt, Andalousia, Morocco, or the Ghana Empire. They came to enroll in courses at the University of Sankore. At its height, the town hosted more than twenty-five thousand students. On parchment, sheepskin, even the scapula of a camel, all that was known was recorded and analyzed. The scribes improvised with writing style inspired by Maghrebi, a form of Arabic script enabling them to economize the use of paper. They wrote descriptions of trading routes for salt and spices, legal writs, sales receipts, pharmacopeia handbooks (including a tract on the harmful effects of tobacco), advice on sexual relations, grammar and mathematics handbooks.

When the Songhay Empire collapsed in the 17th century, these manuscripts were stored away in rusty canisters and dusty cellars, corroded by salt and sand. In time, they came to be forgotten.

*

But for some time now, the silence has been broken. Locals began to talk among themselves. Then, in 1980, there was news from Geneva of trafficking in manuscripts stolen from Timbuktu and sold in New York for "their weight in gold." Whether or not these stories were true, hearing them caused the people of Mali and elsewhere in the diaspora to break their silence. The conversation started in Timbuktu. Thousands of families began to ask themselves why for so many generations they had kept vast quantities of manuscripts in rusty canisters in the most obscure corners of their homes. The people of Sub-Saharan Africa too, especially in Mali, finally began to speak up. All wondered where the manuscripts that they owned had come from. Why was so little known about them? Finally, the outside world joined in the conversation. The scientific information they sought would no doubt upset American, South African, and European historians. For it was a well-established "fact" that the only history that mattered on the Black continent was its oral history.

In one site alone, the city of the "333 saints" (from an excerpt of the *Tarikh al-Sudan* on Timbuktu's origins, p. 36), it is estimated that about a hundred thousand manuscripts exist today. In the vicinity of Timbuktu, there are probably more than three hundred thousand manuscripts in existence. More broadly, throughout a region that includes a portion of the Niger River and extends from Walata to Gao into Arawan, Jenne, and Segu, recognized Malian historians like Mahmoud Zouber estimate that some nine hundred thousand of these manuscripts from the 8th century to the present are still in existence. More significant than these shockingly large figures is the fact that knowledge of them has emerged in direct proportion to the willingness of local families, who were encouraged by government agencies, to empty the contents of their storage bins and at last provide direct access to their family libraries (such as the frequently patronized Kati Family Library in Timbuktu). Others confided their family collections to the Ahmad Baba Institute, an archival center created in 1973 under the authority of UNESCO and the direction of Mahmoud Zouber, cited above.

Among the twenty or so private libraries of Timbuktu, the Mamma-Haidara Library is the most important. No less than nine thousand manuscripts, often of a religious character, are housed there, the oldest dating from the 12th century (1114 C.E.), i.e. a period when the Prophet Muhammad's accomplishments were widely celebrated throughout West Africa. In 1990, Abdel Kader Haidara, the son of a scholar from Timbuktu named Mamma (deceased in 1981), decided to dedicate his life to the preservation of his family's manuscripts. He also decided to relocate his family's other library at Bamba, which dated to the 16th century, to the city of Timbuktu. Today, thousands of family manuscripts are now stored, catalogued, secured, and enumerated at the Mamma-Haidara Library. All that remains is their final restoration and translation.

Once that happens, Africa's history will certainly be rewritten. It awaits us now in these libraries, its progress hobbling along with the appearance of each new translation, university thesis, or international colloquium. A quick glimpse at the massive amount of unpublished material available in these libraries is sufficient to encourage us to believe that it will be possible one day to write an untold story in which Africa will hold a hitherto unimagined place.

But what sense are we to make of everything that has been forgotten? Why has the rediscovery of these manuscripts been so slow and so late in coming? And what should we say now about the myth of Timbuktu fabricated in the abyss of our ignorance? What does this rediscovery tell us about Europe's hostility to anyone who dares to question its dogmatic views about the universality of Greco-Roman philosophy? And what do we make of the fact that Africans too tend to oppose any suggestion whatsoever that their griots, as repositories of oral culture, may not – after all -- be the most reliable safeguards of Africa's traditions? How can we explain the surprising indifference to African writing of 19th explorers, as well as that of 20th century colonizers from Europe? How was it possible that René Caillié neither saw nor heard word of these manuscripts during his stay at Timbuktu? How is it possible that after France occupied Timbuktu at the end of 1894 so little reference was made to this great mass of manuscripts, despite their obvious historical importance? Why was it that the French were only aware of the relatively few archives pillaged by Colonel Archinard after the fall of Segu, and later taken to France where they were deposited in the National Library?

And how can we explain the indifference today of African peoples themselves to learn through translation the meaning of these "African manuscripts written with Arabic characters"? Why is it that, seven centuries later, the political significance of the appearance of writing on the furthest bend of the Niger River is still denied? There is no doubt some historical relation between the collapse of the Songhay Empire in the 17th century (following the Moroccan invasion) and the collective denial of this written memory today in the hearts and minds of those who live in the vicinity of Timbuktu.

*

Around 500 B.C.E. Herodotus first sought to sketch out the broad contours of Africa's civilization. Much later, the Senegalese historian Cheik Anta Diop and the German historian Leo Frobenuis followed in his steps. It is nonetheless evident that we have only a vague notion of this universal history today. In fact, we know next to nothing about it.

When African civilization was even referenced at all, those who dealt with this arbitrarily and invariably severed Africa from Egypt. Bonaparte, the first of many "brilliant" French Egyptologists, then spread the rumor that Egypt's obelisk and hieroglyphs were somehow the historical and cultural "inventions" of the West.

Sometime in the 15th century, the Old Continent cast its gaze upon the New World as Europe's princes began to channel their lust for conquest upon the triangular commerce in slaves. In time, they turned their backs altogether on the Islamic Mediterranean basin. Europe's philosophers too *de facto* eliminated African thought from their speculative field (as happened with Hegel who, in 1830, decreed that "African thought [was] at best the primal stammering of a humanity shrouded in the dark cloak of night"). And so, the die was cast.

During the Enlightenment, it was already forgotten that Holy Roman Church housed an erudite *Description of Africa*, written in the time of the Renaissance by an Arab traveller and convert to Christianity named Leo Africanus (his name at birth was Hassan Ibn Muhammad Al Wasar Al Fassi), who had made the trip to Timbuktu. The rise to power of a pre-capitalist industrial society in Europe further reinforced the *idée recue* that the Black continent did not merit comparison with the West.

Worst still, at the end of the 19th century, widely admired figures like the novelist Victor Hugo (who stated in 1879 that, "during the 19th century, the Negro had finally become a man, thanks to the White Man"), or the philosopher Lucien Lévy-Bruhl. Both were willing collaborators in the creation of a racial hierarchy in which Africans were situated on the lowest rung as "primitives." In their respective areas of inquiry, Marcel Mauss, Maurice Delafosse, and Claude Lévi-Strauss were the best-known representatives of this new ethnographic and anthropological science. And yet, the more prestigious this discipline became over the years, the less Africa came to be known for what it actually was.

*

The manuscripts of Timbuktu force us to reexamine our understanding of the world as we know it. The cataloguing and translation of "The Histories of Timbuktu" by Professor Georges Bohas, founder of the VECMAS program[1] (see appendix, p. 180), illustrate far better than any academic thesis the fecundity of the African imagination in the feudal era; they also reveal even more starkly the profundity of our ignorance about entire generations of African peoples. Whose fault is this? The Afro-American philosopher Kwame Anthony Appiah (*In My Father's House: African in the Philosophy of Culture*, Harvard University Press, 1992) does not follow the lead of his contemporaries, black and white alike, in ignoring the obvious fact that "Black African Muslims have, from time immemorial, enjoyed a long history of writing."

We know today that there exists a copious amount of rare manuscripts containing legal, proprietorial, mathematical, artistic, political, climatological, religious, pharmacological, or medicinal knowledge. Their epistemological worth is such that they are certain to sound the death knoll of our final prejudices about African civilization. Still, it is evident that a massive number of researchers will need to be mobilized in order to restore and translate these manuscripts.

But as we undertake this enormous task in the restoration of cultural memory, we may very well run a certain risk. This risk lies in the troubling tendency among our public officials, both nationally and internationally, to cling to the narrow values of their own cultural heritages. This is the spirit of our times. We are too often bound to serve the *status*

1. VECMAS: "Valorisation et Édition Critique des Manuscrits Subsahariens" (Development, Editing, and Criticism of Sub-Saharan Manuscripts). Along with the Director of the Mamma-Haidra Library, Professor Georges Bohas of the ENS Lyon was also one of the first to point out the need for a program that might insure that future young scholars, who were trained in translation and editing, could continue this important line of research.

quo of our own circumstances and profit from them however we can. From this laziness comes the refusal, or perhaps lack of will, to reform our obviously corrupt scholarly and university systems. Is it possible that our institutions of higher learning are incapable of transmitting this precious cultural heritage? Should this be the case, the most honorable of our scholarly ambitions would come to be abandoned: the dream that is still within our power to reimagine the entire framework of our so-called "universal civilization," a notion that was held in such high esteem by the poet-president Léopold Sédar Senghor.

The Arrival of Caillié, Barth, and Dubois at Timbuktu

René Caillié in 1828

"At last we happily arrived in Timbuktu, just as the sun set along the horizon. I therefore beheld this Sudanese capital, which for so long had been the object of my desires. Upon entering this marvelous city, the focus of so much inquiry among the civilized nations of Europe, I was seized by an inexpressible feeling of satisfaction: I had never before experienced a sensation like it, and my joy was extreme [...]

When my enthusiasm abated, I found that the spectacle before my eyes was not at all what I had expected; I had formed a wholly different idea of the grandeur and wealth of this town: at first glance, it seemed little more than a mass of mud houses, poorly constructed. In every direction, an immense plain of shifting sands, white streaked with yellow, and the greatest aridity unfolded before me. The sky along the horizon was pale red. All of nature seemed sad, and the greatest silence reigned there. You could not hear the singing of a single bird. And yet, there was something inexpressibly imposing about this great town built in the midst of sand. You could not help but admire the efforts of those who had founded it."

Journal of A Voyage To Timbuktu and To Jenne in Central Africa, 1830.

"View of the village of Timbuktu from the summit of an eastern hill." Engraving made from the writing pad of René Caillié's journal, published in 1830.

Heinrich Barth in 1853

"I had at last attained the goal of my difficult enterprise: but from the first hours of my arrival at Timbuktu, I was increasingly certain that it would not be given to me to enjoy in perfect repose of body and spirit the victory that I had won over the difficulties and dangers of the long road that I just traveled. The constant excitement resulting from the incessant delays, as much as my uncertainties about the future of my enterprise, had sustained my faltering health until my arrival at Timbuktu; but from the moment I reached my goal, nearly the very moment that I set my foot in my new house, I was racked with a violent fever; just as the necessity for spiritual and physical resources were never more urgent for me [...]

I made myself at home in the most comfortable fashion possible, and as I did not dare to leave, I often went for fresh air on the terrace of my house. Since I enjoyed there a broad view of the horizon, I tried my best to identify the main features of the town. Towards the south and south-east, my view was admittedly limited by the beautiful houses of the rich Ghadamsi merchants of the Sanegoungou quarter, whereas on the south-west side, I could not see either the Grand Mosque or the Sidi Yahia Mosque; on the other hand, I was able to see the most interesting aspects of the entire north quarter, from the imposing Sakore Mosque and well into the desert extending to the east of the town. When I was not taking air on my terrace, I worked on my travel journal or wrote to my friends in Europe. Naturally, I informed them of my fortuitous arrival in the celebrated village."

Voyages and Discoveries in North and Central Africa, During the Years 1849-1855, Book IV, 1861.

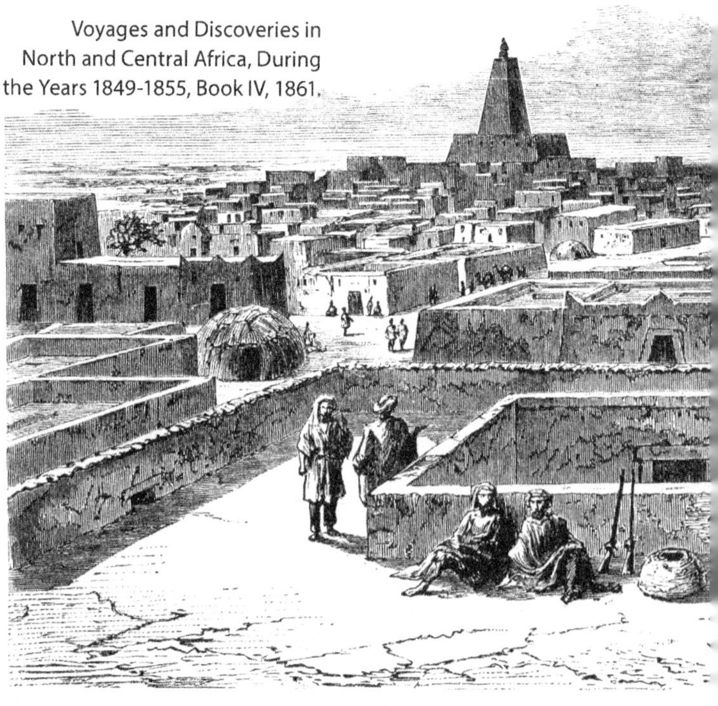

Félix Dubois in 1896

"[Timbuktu] a throne on the horizon, majestic as a queen. It was very much the city that I had imagined, the Timbuktu of Europe's age-old legends. [...] We came to the entrance of the town. Here, the impressive sight that I'd seen suddenly disappeared, like a prop upon a theater stage. A new picture appeared before my eyes. It too made a great impression upon me though mostly by its tragic character. [...]

"And so this was Timbuktu the Great? Timbuktu, the metropolis of the Sahara and the Sudan, so celebrated for its wealth and commerce? This was Timbuktu, the holy city, the center of great learning, this light of the Niger, about which so much has been written: "One day we will correct the texts of our Greek and Latin classics from the manuscripts that are preserved there." Did the secret of Timbuktu the Mysterious lie amid these ruins, the rubble of this town?

"But time passed, and the gaze of the journalist underwent yet another transformation, altering these deceptive first impressions. A steady stream of scholars visited him at his house. One after another, he heard their stories about the Timbuktu chronicles of old:

"The dreary spectacle at my first arrival, which my memory had preserved and which I believed to be unalterable, now grew blurred, dissipating little by little. Timbuktu the Mysterious was obviously shrouded in some great secret. But, I had the eyes to see it. Now, a new vision, one that was quite different, gently took shape before my eyes. At last I saw that great town for what it was, rich and erudite as described in the legends of old."

Timbuktu, The Mysterious,
Flammarion, 1897

General view of Timbuktu. Drawn by Lancelot, from Barth's description.

The Founding of Timbuktu

"This village was founded by Maghcharen Tuaregs at the end of the 5th century of the Hijra. They came into these lands to graze their herds. During the summer season, they camped along the shore of the Niger in the village of Amadagha. In autumn, they would leave once again and head for Araouan where they stayed. This was their furthermost limit in the highlands region. At last, they chose the site of this exquisite, pristine village, the place where we now reside, a lovely and illustrious city that is blessed, lavish, and full of life – my homeland, the most precious thing in the world to me.

Timbuktu has never been sullied by the cult of idols: on its own soil, no one has ever kneeled before Clement. It is the retreat of the scholars and the devout, the preferred residence of saints and all pious men.

From its earliest days, it was here that travelers would meet one another, some coming over land and some on water. They turned this place into a warehouse for their utensils and grains. Soon it became the stopping point of travelers passing through, those coming and going. They entrusted their goods to a slave woman named Timbuktu, a word in the language of the land that means "old woman." It was from her that this blessed place took its name.

Much later, Timbuktu became a place to reside. By the will of God, its population grew. People came from all manner of lands and towns. Soon it became a center of commerce. The first people to come in great numbers were from Ouagadou. They came for commercial purposes. Then merchants from all the neighboring regions began to arrive.

In previous times, Biro was the center of commerce. Travelers came to Biro in streams of caravans from every land imaginable. Great scholars, pious persons, wealthy people of all races and from all lands resided there: they came from Egypt, Audjela, Fezzan, Ghadames, Tuat, Dra, Tafilalet, Fez, Sous, Bitou, etc.

Little by little, all of them relocated to Timbuktu. Finally, all of them lived there."

Tarikh al-sudan, by Abderrahmane Al Sa'di

Heinrich Barth, German explorer of Africa.

Heinrich Barth like Félix Dubois relied upon the Tarikh al-sudan of Abderrahmane Al Sa'di to narrate the history of Timbuktu's founding.

Heinrich Barth discovered this exceptional document in an obscure corner of the Djinbareber Mosque, and Félix Dubois brought it back with him to France in 1896.

"The good fortune was reserved to me to discover this complete history of the Songhay kingdom, dating from the year 1640 of our era. The manuscript was a big tome that was divided into 4 parts. Unfortunately, it was impossible for me to carry a copy of the entire manuscript to Europe, so during my stay at Gando I had to content myself with copying the passages that I considered to be the most significant from the vantage point of history and geography. I used these excerpts, along with other materials assembled, and the conclusions drawn from my own observations of this place, in composing a sufficiently complete chronicle of the Songhay kingdom and its neighboring States."

This chronicle, written in Arabic, was the work of a scholar, who was born May 28, 1596 at Timbuktu. He served as a jurist and was the imam of the Sankore Mosque. The title of Katib, or Secretary of the Government, was bestowed upon him, no doubt for his role as mediator for the diverse princes of the Sudan. These chronicles, which end in the year 1655, consecrate a long chapter to Timbuktu's founding.

The Sankore Mosque of Timbuktu

[illegible] النقل [illegible]

[illegible] سكون الشاعر المتلبس اما الانفصال [illegible]

[illegible] عن سعيد بن جابر [illegible] وقال [illegible]

[illegible] قبل البيت [illegible] فقال [illegible] الرجل جولة [illegible] ولاذ

[illegible] بين كيف على مثلها [illegible] او اوبته [illegible] فقال اعد الكلام وقال [illegible]

[illegible] فقال له تسألني او اسألك فقال له سيبويه بل سل انت [illegible]

[illegible] فاذا هو هي ولا يجوز النصب [illegible] عن امثال ذلك [illegible] خرجت فاذا عبد الله القائم

[illegible] بالرفع فقال له الكسائي العرب ترفع كل ذلك وتنصب فقال يحيى قد اختلفتما

[illegible] فقال الكسائي هذه العرب ببابك [illegible]

[illegible] فقالوا [illegible] الكسائي واستكان سيبويه [illegible]

[illegible] فخرج الى [illegible] فاقام [illegible] حتى مات ولم يعد الى البصرة [illegible]

[illegible] الكسائي عند الرشيد وقال انهم انما [illegible]

[illegible] وان سيبويه قال يحيى [illegible] ان [illegible]

[illegible] ابو الحسن حازم بن محمد الانصاري

SCHOLARSHIP AT THE HEART OF THE SONGHAY EMPIRE

The Birth of the Empire

The first traces of Arabic writing were found not far from Timbuktu, in Gao to be precise. According to Constant Hamès of the Practical School of Advanced Studies, they were spotted on stele grave markers dedicated to personages forgotten by the oral tradition. The grave markers described them as "royals" who had lived in the 11th century.

This is precisely the era when Islam definitively made its way into Africa from the desert. The Senhaja, who were Berbers from the north, brought it to the region. They were the first to come into contact with the Arabs. In 1035, their chief Yahia Ibn Ibrahim visited Mecca and returned with a holy man named Abdullah Yassine. At first, this effective and charismatic preacher was met with great resistance when he sought to convert the Berbers to Islam. He launched his civilizing work from a hermitage along the Atlantic shore, not far from Senegal. According to the Burkinabe historian Joseph Ki Zerbo, these Senhaja (or Lemtouna) founded a capital named Aoudaghost, near Oualata, where the chief, a certain Tinezoua, "assumed authority as the heir of 18 black kings."

Under the name of Al Morabethin (the Almoravids), and with the help of their ally Abu Bakr Ibn Umar, they colonized the wealthy State of Ghana as well as all the lands that bordered Ghana, as far north as Gao, the capital of the Songhay Empire; however, they did not succeed in gaining control of Gao.

From this era dates the fratricidal and recurring wars between the northern and southern regions of the Sahara. "These bloody conflicts had, during times of war and peace, multiplied contacts between the two races and contributed on a daily basis to the reinforcement of the basic traits of the black populations of the Sudan."[1]

A legend narrated by the historian Henri Bidou[2] nicely sums up the origins of this "hybridity" that transformed Timbuktu into such a seismic ground of tribal conflict. At the epicenter of this conflict, its rulers dreamed of overcoming the many racial rivalries in the region.

One day two foreign adventurers who were brothers arrived in this land. The astonished blacks of the region beheld white men for the first time. They asked them their names, but the travelers did not understand. At last, the younger

1. O. Meynier, *L'Afrique noire*. Flammarion, 1914.

2. *L'Afrique*, Flammarion, 1944.

of the two spoke up, motioning to his older brother: He said that his brother came from the Orient. *Dja men al-Yemen.* Due to phonetic differences in the African language, they called the older brother *Za al-Ayaman.* At this time, the Songhay were animists. The devil sometimes appeared before them in the form of a fish that surfaced from the water below. He wore a ring in his nose and gave commands to them. Za al-Ayaman, who was a Muslim, killed the fish with his spear and the people made him their new king.

There is no doubt some historical truth to this legend: several white nomads, after a few adventures crossing the Sahara, took refuge among the Songhay where they assumed power. Jacques Béraud-Villars deduces from this legend that it obviously refers to the Tuareg. From that day forward, the Songhay became a proletariat of black farmers ruled by a white aristocracy. Many diverse ethnic groups then settled in the "Land of the Blacks," including among the Mande who established the Empire of Mali. Mosques were now built and, even if – as the learned traveler Ibn Battuta noted in his *Prolegomena* -- indigenous peoples did not show much zeal in supporting the new religion, it is nonetheless true that by the 12th century Islam prevailed and came to be homogenized with more local social practices. On the other hand, Islam barely made a dent on the powerful animist imagination. On the contrary, the Songhay people (but also the Mossi to the east) successfully created a synthesis of an endogenous mode of existence in which local tradition continued to resist the new religion.

It is curious, however, that the traveler Ibn Battuta's written account did not arouse more interest among the educated Arabs of the 14th century. At the time of his visit in 1352, he wrote that Timbuktu's "Sultan has absolutely no tolerance for injustice and neither its inhabitants nor travelers need fear theft or any other form of aggression: everyone lives in perfect security."[3] At this time, it was rare that a feudal state, empire, or monarchy on the peripheries of the Mediterranean might enjoy such a high degree of social serenity in their lands. Already then, we begin to sense a nascent arrogance towards this "indistinct" Africa, construed as vaguely black but too well organized to be classified in every instance as primitive.

Upon the urging of the caliphs of Egypt and the emirs of the Maghreb, the Songhay sovereign Kankan Musa visited Mecca in 1325 to legitimate his reign. At this historical juncture, it is likely that the people of this region were invested in the creation of their own history, which they knew was unlike any other.

This "wise king" left on horseback to accomplish his pilgrimage, escorted by forty mules loaded down with gold, a retinue of fifty thousand followers, preceded by five hundred slaves, each carrying a golden rod weighing more than

3. *L'Empire de Gao*, Plon, 1942.

three kilos (five hundred *mitsqals*). Upon his arrival, it was clear to the peoples of the Middle East that Kankan Musa's Empire lacked their same zeal for the canonical doctrines of Islam, as they were taught in "North Africa," particularly in Egypt.

The King of Songhay, like a prince from the *Thousand and One Nights*, visited the holy city as much to obtain the title of caliph as he did to bring home Asian-made paper, along with the most talented Arab artisans and intellectuals. Upon his return, he had clearly demonstrated that he was able to pay both architects and scholars.

This was how he was succeeded in recruiting the celebrated Ishaq Al Tuedjin, who built the Grand Mosque of Djindaberrer from clay at Timbuktu. It was Al Tuedjin who trained Africa's architects and who invented a Sudanese style of construction with the use of a white stone called *alhor*. This mode of construction has lost none of its popularity in the valley of the Niger today.

The reign of Kankan Musa was followed by the reign of Sunni Ali Ber (1464-1492). The Songhay kingdom expanded and prospered. At Sunni Ali's death, one of his generals rose to power: Al Hajj Muhammad. For more than a century later, the Askiya dynasty ruled the Empire (1493-1592). After the Askiya Muhammad, his oldest son, the Askiya Musa, assumed power, followed by his nephew the Askiya Muhammad Bounkan, and then three of the Askiya Muhammad's sons, the Askiya Ismail, the Askiya Ishaq and, most famously, the Askiya Dawud (1549-1582). The long and prosperous reign of the Askiya Dawud marked the high point of the dynasty. As Octave Meynier wrote, "We believe that at no time and in no other place did there exist in black Africa an indigenous state that was better and more powerfully organized than the Songhay Empire of the 16th century."

And so it happened that the Songhay Empire, the womb of this luminescent Sudanese state, was gradually transformed into an enchanted cultural space where ideas were openly shared and propagated. At the heart of Sub-Saharan Africa, the *ulemas* (from the Arabic *ulama*, one who holds power) were respected, consulted, and assisted. Above all, they were well protected by their emperors, who were sufficiently educated to attract the interest of scholars from all regions. They were also shrewd enough to surround themselves with men of letters to advise them.

A manuscript from the 17th century. The first page of a book by Al Jazuli, deceased in 1465.

بسم الله الرحمن الرحيم

صلى الله على سيدنا محمد نبيه

واله وصحبه وسلم تسليما

وبه نستعين

قال الشيخ الفقيه الامام
محمد الجزولي رضي الله عنه

الحمد لله الذي هدانا للايمان

والاسلام والصلاة والسلام

سبع سموات وسبع الارض
وما فيها وما

The Convergence of Trade and Knowledge

A quick glance at a map (see p. 12) may help us to better understand the privileged nature of Timbuktu's location on the arc of the Niger. As soon as the Askiya was able to assure the Sahara's security, the interior riches of Africa could be traded for salt extracted from Teghazza, but also firearms, cheap goods, fabrics from Europe, and Berber horses, as well as horses from the Levant, which the Sudanese bought at exorbitant prices.

"Even the lowest quality drapes from Europe sold for four ducats, fifteen at mid-range, and those from Venice, of finely woven scarlet, blue, and violet sold for not less than thirty ducats," Leo Africanus wrote in 1526. The Songhay nobles did not resist the temptation to acquire such luxuries. In fact, this was how "they got into debt with the Maghrabian and Levantian merchants who were established in the Tekrur, the descendants of Syrians, who one will find still residing in West Africa," Beraud-Villars notes in his history of the Sudanese Empire, written in 1942. "In reality, the towns of the middle Niger River, particularly Timbuktu, had become centers of finance and speculation," he adds. Contracts were negotiated with merchants in Fez, Kairouan, Venice, Gènes, and Cairo, but those who did so wanted to obtain, once their business was concluded, a written receipt; in other words, they wanted documented proof of their transactions. Discount and exchange rates were commonly discussed. Depending upon the quantity of gold imported from Bambouk, the value of the cowrie (used as money in the interior) would rise or fall. Goods of European origin, but salt too on a grander scale, were paid for in gold. (Written bills of sale are preserved at the Mamma-Haidara Library.)

At the apex of the Songhay Empire, the main routes leading out of Timbuktu headed towards the northern, eastern, and western regions of Africa. The regular caravans that traveled these routes enjoyed complete security due to an array of Tuareg and Moor caravans that specialized in this type of traffic. After having long regarded the Sudan as a natural extension of North Africa, historians writing in Arabic began at this time to discuss the "Land of the Blacks" as a distinct place.

From this time forward, a truly trans-Saharan commerce began to take root at Timbuktu, extending across West and East Africa without regard for the North. The commerce based at Timbuktu played a role in Africa's evolution by attracting scholars and facilitating a dynamic and unprecedented era of intellectual prosperity.

The contents of an open suitcase at a family library in Timbuktu.

The Force of the Law

From the beginning of its history until the French conquered it in 1894, Timbuktu was administered according to the precepts of the Maliki (named for a jurist from Tuat). The most prominent advocates of this school of Islamic law were Ahmad Baba and Ahmad Al Bakkay among others.

The *qadi* is the incarnation of law and justice. Appointed for life by the emperor, his role was to help maintain the balance of power by legally protecting the citizens of Timbuktu against the arbitrariness and tyranny of its rulers. For instance, at the Mama Haidara Library there is a handwritten manuscript by a *qadi* on the emancipation of a slave who was mistreated by his master.

Assisted by secretaries, bailiffs, and notaries, these men of letters, drafted from the town's most prominent families, were able to assure the existence of the civil state merely through their service as judges. The inestimable rulings or legal notices that are amply documented in the manuscripts attest to this fact. Matters involving the exercise of more traditional forms of justice were consigned to the authority of the local chiefs, who normally acted in good faith and with discretion.

To obviate all forms of bureaucracy – the defining characteristic of modern forms of public management – the *qadi* was not allowed to delegate his authority. The Norwegian geographer Benjaminsen and his colleague in socio-anthropology Berge studied this question for many years (*Une histoire de Tombouctou*, Actes Sud, 2004). They concluded that "to have conceived of such a system and put it into place beforehand insured that the conditions of corruption could not exist. *Qadis* were chosen who lived in comfortable financial circumstances. Regardless of the impact upon the civil state, the *qadi* alone bore responsibility for his actions. The absence of appointed subordinates meant that the legal propriety of his decisions would not be subjected to undue suspicions."

This well documented analysis of the *Tarikh al-sudan* demonstrates the high level of political maturity that the Songhay had attained in the 15th century.

Another exceptional document reinforces Benjaminsen and Berge's analysis, Mahmud Kati's *Tarikh al-fattash*, which was discovered fourteen years after Barth happened upon the *Tarikh al-sudan*.

Hence, for nearly two centuries, this civilization was organized and developed in accordance with a highly developed system of law and justice. The chronicler of the *Tarikh al-fattash* documents its prosperity:

"Timbuktu was unparalleled among the various towns in the lands of the Blacks for the solidity of its institutions, its political liberties, moral purity, the security of its citizens and their property, mercy and compassion towards strangers, the courtesy extended to students and men of science, as well as the assistance it provided to them."

None of this could have happened without the existence of a written justice system, as the rediscovered manuscripts vividly illustrate. The educated classes ceaselessly updated and discussed the manuscripts, including the judges (*fuquaha*) who were representatives of the political elites and the *ulemas* who were representatives of the middle class. The steady production of these texts shows how this scholarly coupling guaranteed a minimal level of democratic participation. In a manuscript dating from 1615, for instance, we find several "treaties on good governance" and on "the emancipation of slaves" for diplomatic ends and for the benefit of "men of power" (from a manuscript in bad condition restored in the 19th century and now held at the Ahmad-Baba Library).

As happened in Celtic Europe in the 15th century, when Druids served as priests, judges, and scholars in Christian lands, the "bards" (griots) of the 15th century took their place among the *ulemas* in the Islamic lands of black animist Africa. Never had so many stories been written and new legends invented.

This was the inevitable outcome of the Songhay's fascination for learning, art, and – above all – writing. In opposition to those who cast aspersion upon the very idea of traditional African civilization, the cultural awakening that took place among the Songhay offers conclusive evidence of a humanist tradition in Africa.

The *Tarikh al-fattash*[1]

Fourteen years after the discovery of the Tarikh al-sudan by Heinrich Barth, another chronicle, the Tarikh al-fattash, was discovered in the personal library of a scholar from Timbuktu. The discovery was made by Bonnel de Mézières, a Frenchman acting on behalf of the governor of Upper Senegal-Niger, Francois Joseph Clozel. This remarkable written account ended in 1599, but it gave further credibility to the historical account of the Sudan documented in the first *Tarikh*. It also enriched our historical understanding of the region. Another scholar from Timbuktu signed his name to this volume, Mahmud Kati.

The author of the *Tarikh al-fattash* was a Black man of Wakuri origins who belonged to a family of letters from Kurima (a village to the west of Timbuktu). He was born in 1468 during the era of Sunni Al Ber's ascendency to the Songhay throne. He was a member of the small circle of devotees who took their place at the side of the future emperor Askiya Muhammad in 1497 when he took the hajj to Mecca, like so many of his predecessors. Kati performed the functions of a *qadi* and had also earned the title of *alfa*, a doctor or legal advisor, due to his reputation as a man of science. Mahmud Kati died when he was more than a hundred years old, but not before he confided the task of completing this unprecedented history of the Songhay empire to one of his grandsons.

This chronicle is therefore a document of "the first rank in understanding the history of the Sudan. It provides a host of precise information on the political, administrative, and social organization of lands of the Niger prior to the Moroccan conquest at the end of the 16th century.

"Its general subject is revealed in the phrase from its full title: It is a collection of documents gathered to facilitate research into the history and origins of the towns and kingdoms of the Sudan, its principle dynasties and tribes, whether noble or servile, major military expeditions and their consequences, as well as the most remarkable personages of these lands. Above all, its authors seek to recount the

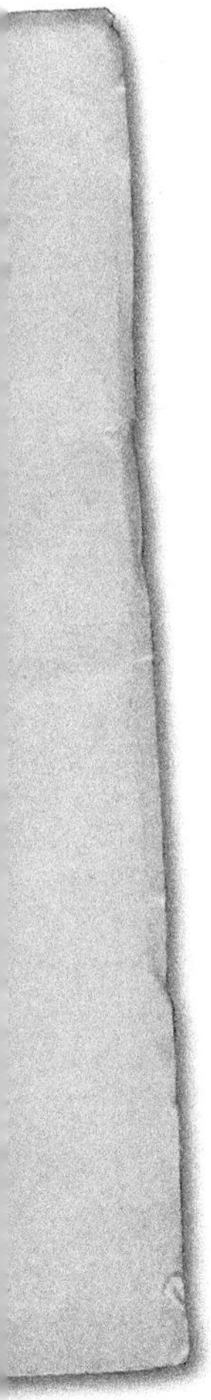

history and organization of the Songhay Empire under the dynasty of the Askiya of Gao, from the reign of Al Hajj Muhammad (1493-1529) to the Moroccan conquest (1591)."

Among the remarkable personalities of the Empire, Mahmud Kati introduces us to the famous scholar Ahmad Baba as well as the dialogue that took place between him and the Sultan of Morocco, Mulay Ahmad Al Mansour. At this time, the sultan had imprisoned Timbuktu's most prestigious scholar at Marrakech.

Not long after the sultan conquered and massacred many Songhay people in order to gain the Sahel's highly coveted wealth, the scholar openly questioned the sultan's motives:

"Why did you need to plunder all my goods and pillage nearly two thousand of my books?" he asked. "What was the point of putting me in irons and bringing me here?"

"We wanted to foster Muslim unity in the world," Mansour responded.

"Why didn't you foster unity among the Tlemchen Turks instead? Their lands are closer to you than our lands."

Those who dared to speak so boldly before the Sultan were usually killed on the spot by his royal guard. But the black *ulemas* were held in such high esteem in Morocco, especially Ahmad Baba, that the Sultan did not even punish them. Even more surprisingly, Ahmad Baba continued to teach during the entire time of his imprisonment at the request of his scholarly colleagues in the Sultan's court. Fifteen years later, Ahmad Baba was granted his request to return to Timbuktu where he wanted to end his days.

This historical episode provides evidence of the unique and advanced nature of African knowledge at this time, especially in the case of Ahmad Baba, but also all the *ulemas* of Timbuktu, Jenne, Gao, who had no need to immerse themselves in the encyclopedic learning traditions of Fez or Marrakech. They were black scholars and quite proud of the fact.

1. Mahmud Kati's *Tarikh al-fattash*, Maisonneuve

COLLECTION U. N. E. S. C. O. D'ŒUVRES REPRÉSENTATIVES SÉRIE AFRICAINE

PUBLICATIONS DE L'ÉCOLE DES LANGUES ORIENTALES VIVANTES

DOCUMENTS ARABES RELATIFS A L'HISTOIRE DU SOUDAN

TARIKH ES-SOUDAN

PAR

ABDERRAHMAN BEN ABDALLAH BEN 'IMRAN BEN 'AMIR ES-SA'DI

TEXTE ARABE ÉDITÉ ET TRADUIT

PAR

O. HOUDAS

PROFESSEUR A L'ÉCOLE DES LANGUES ORIENTALES VIVANTES

Avec la collaboration de

Edm. BENOIST

Élève diplômé de l'École des langues orientales vivantes.

LIBRAIRIE D'AMÉRIQUE ET D'ORIENT

Adrien MAISONNEUVE

J. MAISONNEUVE, succ.

11, rue St-Sulpice

PARIS

1981

Excerpt from the *Tarikh al-sudan*

About the Scholar *Ahmad Baba*

"The jurist, the scholar, the very learned, the crown jewel, and most exceptional man of his time, the most remarkable scholar in all branches of science, was Abu-Abbas-Ahmad-Baba, son of the jurist Ahmad-Ibn-Al-Hajj-Umar-Ibn-Muhammad-Aqit.

He demonstrated the greatest zeal and most lively intelligence from the earliest days of his studies, standing out among all his contemporaries and greatly exceeding them. He alone debated the sciences with his masters, and they bore witness to the extent of his knowledge. His valor was celebrated in the Maghreb and his renown spread very far. All the doctors in the great villages recognized his superiority in the matter of fatwa. He upheld the most rigorous standards of justice, even towards the most humble of men; he spoke out about all matters of justice before the emirs and sultans."

Later, the Tarikh makes reference to one of Ahmad Baba's works, Edz-Dzil. In this same place, the scholar describes his grandfather:

"As a jurist, lexicographer, grammarian, writer, and scholar, he occupied himself with learning his entire life. His books were vast and were annotated with numerous handwritten comments. At the time of his death, he left around seven hundred volumes."

■

Questions for Egyptian Scholars [1]

This document is entitled *masail ila ulamai misra*, meaning "questions for Egyptian scholars." It contains twenty-one questions that Ahmad Baba addressed to the *ulemas* of Egypt. These questions address many different areas of inquiry: the granting of prayer wishes on the specific day of Friday, according to the views of various *haji's* (traditions of the prophet cited on this subject), but also law, ethics, theology, and syntax. The text was written in 1605.

Among the questions included are the following: What is your point of view about soothsayers and those who say that there are days of the year that bring good fortune and days that bring disasters? On the other hand, should one be wary of undertaking an ambitious project, or any project where one hopes to succeed, on certain ill-fated days? ...

What is your advice regarding those who follow the views of the great Shaykh Abu Al Abas Al Bouni regarding magic and talismans? Should one press them into service for one's needs, and even delight in them, despite the fact that doing so necessitates engaging the sciences of astronomy and "the mystical gravity of letters?" Furthermore, to take full advantage of this opportunity, we also ask you if the "science of mystical gravity" is a new science or if it existed during the time of the first companions of the prophet? And what about the miracles of the saints? Also, what are your views regarding magic and the impact of certain supernatural things, taking into account the providence of Allah and given the hypothesis "that there is nothing without reason"?

What can be known regarding the state of the soul, given the particularly of our emotions, the real nature of the heart, and scientific motion that attracts, such as enamel and iron?

■

1. *Masail ila ulamai misra*, Author: Ahmad Baba Ibn Ahmad Ibn Al Hajj Ahmad Ibn Umar Ibn Muhammad Ibn Aqui Al Tinbukti Al-Sudani (October 26, 1556 – April 22, 1627). Bnf Arab: 5382, f. 62v. – 72v.

Studies of Manuscripts on *fatwa* and *nazila*, dating from the 19th Century

By Mohamed Hamady
University of Nouakchott

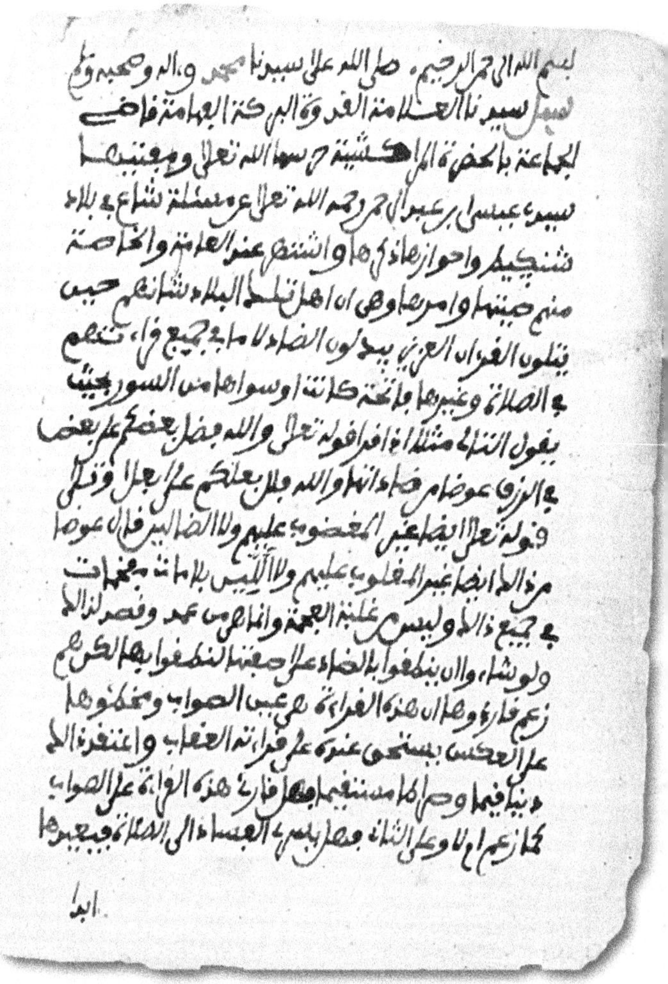

The fatwa is a legal opinion written by a scholar of high repute in order to clarify already established legal viewpoints and juridical rulings.

On the other hand, whenever one speaks of the *nazila* (literally "calamity"), it refers to an unusual situation during which a scholar of high repute is consulted to analyze the law and articulate an appropriate respond to a case without precedent.

What is most interesting about the collections of *fatwa* and *nazila* is the variety of the subjects that they address. This enables us to reconstruct the general situation underwriting their composition. The scientific and literary quality of these works proves, should there be need for it, the high degree of culture attained by African societies at this time. Admittedly, these *fatwas* also reveal the steady degradation of social and political conditions, including public safety, even as they demonstrate the fabulous cultural heritage that these manuscripts have come to symbolize today.

The degradation of knowledge and loss of literacy were so significant that we have recently discovered works in manuscript form among black American families, inherited from ancestors who were deported to the Americas in the era of the trans- Atlantic slave trade. Of course, their descendants have no idea what is written in these manuscripts, but the past generations that brought these writings with them were obviously highly educated people who were sold as common slaves.

In other words, Africa was a highly developed civilization with a complex written history, precisely at the moment that other societies sought to turn its people into their slaves. The collection of *fatwas* presented here aptly illustrates this historical situation. A portion of a text of great literary and scientific merit is presented here, demonstrating the erudition of its author and the level of culture attained in the setting he describes. These *fatwas* equally suggest a wide range of social, political, and economic situations that enable us to gain a sufficiently clear idea of the era that they describe.

This fatwa discusses the existence of a community that pronounces the letter ض in the form of ل L.

Was it because of certain linguistic constraints that it was so difficult for this community to pronounce a letter that existed in Arabic but not in their own language? Why then do the members of this linguistic community continue to assert that their vocalization of this Arabic sound is the correct one?

*

Another original *fatwa* addresses a question posed to the *faqih* regarding an exceptional situation: a woman found herself married to two husbands at the same time. The lady in question was married to the man who she wanted to be her legal guardian. But her father, who was still alive and was her guardian from birth, did not know of the existence of his daughter's unscrupulous suitor; in fact, the father had already married his daughter to entirely different suitor.

The author of the *fatwa* helped find a solution to this unusual situation.

Which of the two men won the "big prize"?

The scholar, while insisting upon the fact that the first marriage had not followed proper social etiquette and so should

Working Documents:
Compilations of *nazila* (legal opinions) by Mbouya Ibn Al Imam of Walata.

A Few Benchmarks:
Volume: 205 pages
Area: Islamic law (*figh*)
Compiler: Mbouya Ibn Al Imam, Walati Scholar (1843)

مسئلتان من اللقطة والضوال

never have taken place, could find no argument to invalidate it now. He therefore recognized the legitimacy of the first marriage, but he also recommended that the authorities impose a fitting punishment upon the suitor who was obviously an expert in skirting the rules of social etiquette.

*

Another question posed to a *faqih* clearly reveals the insecure political situation of the era it was written. The person who poses the question wanted to know if the law of compensation remained applicable given the absence of any centralized power that was capable of applying the law. What is the appropriate response if a person injured another person in a manner that mandated some form of compensation, but the aggressor refused to reciprocate in full measure? In this case, forcing him to do so could lead to a conflict between the tribes of both parties. The author of this legal ruling declares that the next of kin of the victim must agree to accept the amount of compensation that the aggressor could afford to pay, even if the amount was not what is should have been.

به نحو مصعفور عليها الا واو فيه فيه جمعة والمعرفة
فا وجا واحرا وفلا ينسبه من الكا فيه على ذلك
بحوه من الحجر بعضه مفرد من الا عجزه مبنيه حرفان
عمران وعمانا دوا اسما وزيدان ويب ليات علمين وحمون
علمين وتخفيفه وعفريت وعسلس اعلاما ثم اشار
والعجز اخرى من مركب اذا رخم المركب نحوه
به بعلبك وسيبويه وخمسة عشر علما واحمسة
من العدد اذا سمي به ومنع اكثر الكوفيين ترخيم احره
ومنه من كالها فتقول يا سيبو وقال ابن كيسان
كب بان حذفت الحرف والحرفين فقلت يا بعلبك ويا
فقوله الجزء لمي رخم المركب وانما جاز النحويون فيما
وانثى عشرة علمين حذفت العجز مع الالف قبلها
حذفت العجز مع الالف قبله فتقول يا اثن ويا اثنت
كما نص عليه سيبويه وعلته ان عجزهما بمنزلة
ومن ترخيم جملة واذا عمر ونحو قال المصنف
ثم المركب المحكم اسنادا كتابه ثم او سوجا نحو
النسب فقال نقول ذو النسب الذاته ثم اناطهر
منع ترخيمه في باب الترخيم بعلا نه لا ان منع ترخيمه
قال الشارح بعلان ترخيمه بجوازه على الحذف قليلا
من نحو عمرو وبكر وانهم سيبويه هذا الشيخ
سيبويه لم ينص على ترخيمه بل قال من الهمز ان
او معرفا وليس منا فضلا في هذا المحكي
هذا على جهة الترخيم ولكن الاقال سيبويه فرد ولم
نحو بين ان المحكي لا يرخم واعلم ان في الترخيم
الذاتيه ان الاينبو وقد اشار الى الاول بقوله
زه والباقي استعمل بما فيه الفي اذا فرغنا ثبوت
ركبة ما قبله على ما عرف الجزء واشتهر لغته

عليه ... ونقل ... ترخيم المضاف ... بعض العجم

أهمل المصنف من شروط ترخيم المجرد ثلاثة أحدها أن لا يكون مختصا بالنداء
والثاني أن لا يكون مبنيا والثالث أن لا يكون مستغاثا ... أما ...
فلم ينبه عليه وأما الثاني والثالث فقد يفهم ما أرشد إليهما وسوى نصه
على الترخيم حرف النداء معما أن علة الترخيم هي علة منع ترخيمها وأجاز
ابن خروف ترخيم المستغاث إذا لم تكن فيه اللام كقوله أعام لك ابن صعصعة
ابن سعد قال ابن الضائع وهذه ضرورة وقد نادى الشاعر بغير ياء ...
ترخيمه وسمع ... كقوله كلما نادى ... يا لتميم الله ...
اعلم أن الخالي من تاء التأنيث إذا استوفى شروط الترخيم فالمحذوف منه للترخيم
آخره وأما حرفان وأما كلمة فالذي يحذف منه حرف نحو حارث ومالك فتقول
يا حار ويا مال وأما الذي يحذف منه حرفان فقد أشار إليه بقوله ومع الآخر احذف
الذي تلا إن زيد لينا ساكنا مكملا أربعة فصاعدا ... أن يحذف مع الآخر ما قبله
بخمسة شروط ... أن يكون حرف لين فلو كان حرفا صحيحا ... حذف الآخر
وحده فتقول في سفرجل ... يا سفرج ... ويا قمط ... خلافا للفراء ...
فإنه يقول يا قم ... يحذف حرفين الثاني أن يكون ساكنا فلو كان متحركا لم يحذف
فتقول في قنور ... يا قنو ... يحذف الآخر وحده الثالث أن يكون
زائدا فلو كان أصليا لم يحذف فتقول في مختار يا مختا ...
لأنها بدل ... عن الأخفش أنه يحذف مع الآخر وأجاز الجرمي ...
... الرابع أن يكون رابعا فصاعدا فلو كان ثالثا نحو عماد
وسعيد وثمود ... حذف آخره فقط ونقل المصنف عن
... أنه أجاز نحو عماد وسعيد ... حذفه مع الآخر ...
... والياء فتقول يا عم ويا سعي وأما ثمود فيحذف الآخر من
... إلا أن بقاء الواو ... عن الكسائي ونقل غيره عن الفراء أنه
يحذف الآخر ... ثمود ويجوز ... فقط في عماد وسعيد ... يكون قبله
... مجانسة فلو كان قبل الواو والياء فتحة نحو غرنيق وفرعون
... الجرمي والفراء أنه يحذف مع الآخر ... قبله حركة مجانسة ...
... وغيرهما لا يرى ذلك ... يقولون يا فرعو ...
ذهب إليه هو مذهب ... الأكثرين ...

Preceding pages: a treatise and commentary on grammar and linguistics, by the *Alfiyya* Ibn Malik. He addresses a problem referred to as tarhim, "truncation." For example, *Ya Mansu* is sometimes substituted for *Ya Mansuru*. The title of this work is *Tawdih al-maqasid bi-sarhi alfiyyat ibn Malik*. The author is Al Makudi, deceased in 1405. The ink consists of a mixture of powder, carbon, kaolin, and Arabic gum-rubber (end of the 17th century).

Principles of Governance

The considerable mass of documents discovered at Timbuktu also reveals a great deal about the political organization of the Songhay Empire. Obviously, this was a highly sophisticated society from an administrative standpoint. The peace treaties and caveats articulated by the responsible parties are legion. From the time of the 14th century, written treaties were drawn up between black kings: ambassadors would be sent from the literate elite as well as from the military whose diplomatic skills remain unsurpassed in the modern era. Despite the fall of the Songhay Empire in the 17th century, written forms of public negotiation continued to be ever more refined (from a manuscript held at Mama Haidara Library on the subject of the Tuareg). These documents reveal the complexity of formal diplomatic negotiations among Sudanese chiefdoms, which were as every bit as sophisticated as those of our era.

In his *Letter to the People of Macina*, written in 1850, the war chief Al Hajj Umar picked up a calame with his own hand (a writing implement made of reed) to explain the reasons for his dispute with his enemy at that time, Ahmadu Ahmadu. In doing so, he sought to emphasize that the conflict was solely between the king and him, and that he had no quarrel with the local population. The highly diplomatic and subtle point he made was that in matters of intra-African territorial conquest "the people have the right to be kept informed."[1] Hence, in public affairs recourse to picking up the pen was no mere administrative formality, but a cultural practice that took place within a particular political and historical setting. Does it not seem likely that the scruples of Al Hajj Umar in this case would have inspired Machiavelli himself when he offered advice to the powerful of his day in *The Prince*? Could it be that the views of Machiavelli on the exercise of power were more expertly practiced in Africa than they were in Europe?

The most random glimpse at many of these manuscripts (the *Tarikhs* in particular) is sufficient to demonstrate the incontestable political maturity of the Empire's elites. Through the combined (and highly centralized) exercise of religious and political power, they succeeded in building a highly efficient Islamic State. From the inception of the Songhay Empire, its citizens profited from the skills of its leaders and took advantage of the many contributions of their pre-

1. Reported in *Mother Africa*, by Basil Davidson, Puf, 1965.

decessors in building strong institutions. This was particularly true in the case of Sunni Ali Ber, the predecessor of the Askiyas, who was a tyrannical warrior but diabolically inventive in the art of conquering neighboring territories. His successor the Askiya Muhammad knew how to take full advantage of Sunni Ali's conquests through maintaining and consolidating them. He built a centralized empire of two thousand five hundred kilometers, from east to west, and a thousand kilometers, from north to south. In fact, he built an administration that continues to confound researchers today. The fruits of his labor endured until the Moroccans colonized the region at the beginning of the 17th century; they were definitively brought to an end with the arrival of the French in the 19th century.

Zakari Dramani-Issifou, who spent several years investigating the ancient manuscripts of Timbuktu, has remarked on this question:[2]

"Aside from the great power of the emperor and those belonging to his court, as well as that of his ministers and provincial governors, it is the power of the dignitaries that merits the most attention."

Theirs was an honorary responsibility that they exercised apart from any political or administrative hierarchy. It was linked to the skills they possessed and the functions they performed, both as superiors or subordinates. This enabled those who faithfully managed the empire to ascend to the highest degrees of power by virtue of their individual talents. But unlike those who have been awarded the Legion of Honor in France, honored dignitaries among the Songhay could gain an audience with the emperor to whom they could make formal appeals. In point of fact, only dignitaries from the imperial family (very great in number but infiltrating all layers of society) were fully authorized to do so. From the official viewpoint, centralized power in the Empire required reliable informers who could insure the hegemony of its rulers in the most "democratic" manner possible.

The official terminology that they employed demonstrates their high degree of refinement in the art of delegating tasks to more efficiently rule. In effect, the sovereign surrounded himself with the most intelligent dignitaries available who possessed the necessary skills that he required. They included Songhay marabouts, *ulemas*, and *qadis*, but also foreigners (Ibrahim Al Khidr, the personal secretary of Sunni Ali Ber, was originally from Fez). They were jurists and men of letters, all of whom had absorbed the religious and humanist culture characteristic of Timbuktu, Cairo, or Fez. Some warriors or military men who advised the sovereign at Gao, as well as at Timbuktu, but especially in the provinces, were members of the imperial family who, above all, were skilled in the art of "reflecting upon the nature of power and holding onto it."[3]

A written source predating the *Tarikhs* bears witness to the sophistication of the Songhay's political power and the importance accorded to the *res publica* ("public thing"; see Cheikh Hamidou Kane's contribution, p. 24).

"There was a *Mande Oath* (or *Charter*) that was discovered in 1965, as reported by the historian Adame Ba Konare (*Le Monde*, July 2010). In this charter that dates from 1235 and that was written on the occasion of the inauguration of the

2. *L'Afrique noire dans les relations internationales au XVI siècle*, Karthala, 1982.

3. *Timbuktu, The Mysterious*, of Félix Dubois, Flammarion, 1897.

Emperor Sundiata Keita, the founder of the Mali Empire, the peoples of the region swear to uphold a form of social organization that is based upon authentic democratic values: hospitality, or respect for the stranger, respect for one's neighbors, access to justice, philosophical conceptions of tolerance, rights, and duties."

At Jenne and at Gao, but above all at Timbuktu, there were ample oral traditions although writing was introduced very early and was heavily relied upon, as confirmed by Ahmed Chokri in his work on African historiography.[4] After first listening to the ancients, their words were transcribed and then copied, possibly among a group of scholars. It was in the mosques or madrasas where ideas about Islam's interpretation were shared and propagated, in an open and rather generous atmosphere. How else is it possible to explain the discovery and then translation of the ethnologist Youssouf Tata Cisse's rendition of the Mande brotherhood of hunters (from a region south of the modern nation of Mali), a surprising text that demands nothing less than the abolition of slavery?

According to Jacques Le Goff, as Christian Europe in the Medieval period cultivated stereotypes about pagan Blacks and Africa, at the foot of the Dogon cliffs, "standing brigades of Mande hunters ceaselessly hunted down all those who trafficked in slaves..."[5]

In fact, this account from the 13th century, which was discovered and then transmitted by the marabout Fadjima Kante, reflects the humanistic environment that prevailed at the beginning of the Mali Empire, the predecessor to the Songhay Empire. The main values it promotes are tolerance, fraternity, and moral rectitude. What took place at this time was not unlike the early days of the Renaissance in Europe when a return to the values of Greco-Roman Antiquity were first championed. Here is an excerpt from this charter: "As long as we possess a quiver and a bow / famine will kill no one who lives among the Mande / should famine occur / no war will ever destroy our villages ever again / in order to make captives into slaves / from now on no one will ever put / a bit in the mouth of his fellow man / in order to sell him / no one will ever again be beaten among the Mande / or put to death by fiat / because he is the son of a slave."[6]

From the 14th century onward, the notion of the State was solidly anchored in the Empire. The professional army obviously exuded confidence, as its educated officers in the cavalry were reputed to be efficient and highly mobile while policing the region as far as Morocco or even the Middle East. For more than a century, as neighboring empires and the Northern regions were perpetually at war, the Songhay built a state-run organization in black Africa that rivaled all those in Europe and elsewhere. It was founded upon basic principles of human rights and justice and, it must be underscored, a certain understanding of the power of the spirit. In its time, this spirit was fully capable of fostering both Islamic and animist forms of spirituality, as well as a legal and political system that was based upon reason.

Sounding a bit like his famous predecessor Ahmad Baba, one of Timbuktu's last men of letters in the era of the French conquest, Ahmad Al Bakkay, remarked to Benjaminsen that, "the power of the State and the exercise of justice should

4. Institut d'études africaines, Rabat, 2010.

5. *L'Occident et l'Afrique du XIII au XV siècle.* Francois de Medeiros, Kartala, 1985.

6. *La Charte du Mandé*, translated by Youssouf Tata Cisse and Jean-Louis Sagot Duvauroux, Albin Michel, 2003..

never be in the same hands." Today like yesterday, when the head of the Malian State visits Timbuktu, he is the one who must seek out the *qadi* to formally greet him, not the other way around.

On the pages to follow: a calendar of the Muslim months. The lunar calendar: Jumada, Rajah, Ramadan, Chawwal, and Dhu l-hijja. Knowledge of what corresponds to the symbols "o" and the "•" has been lost.

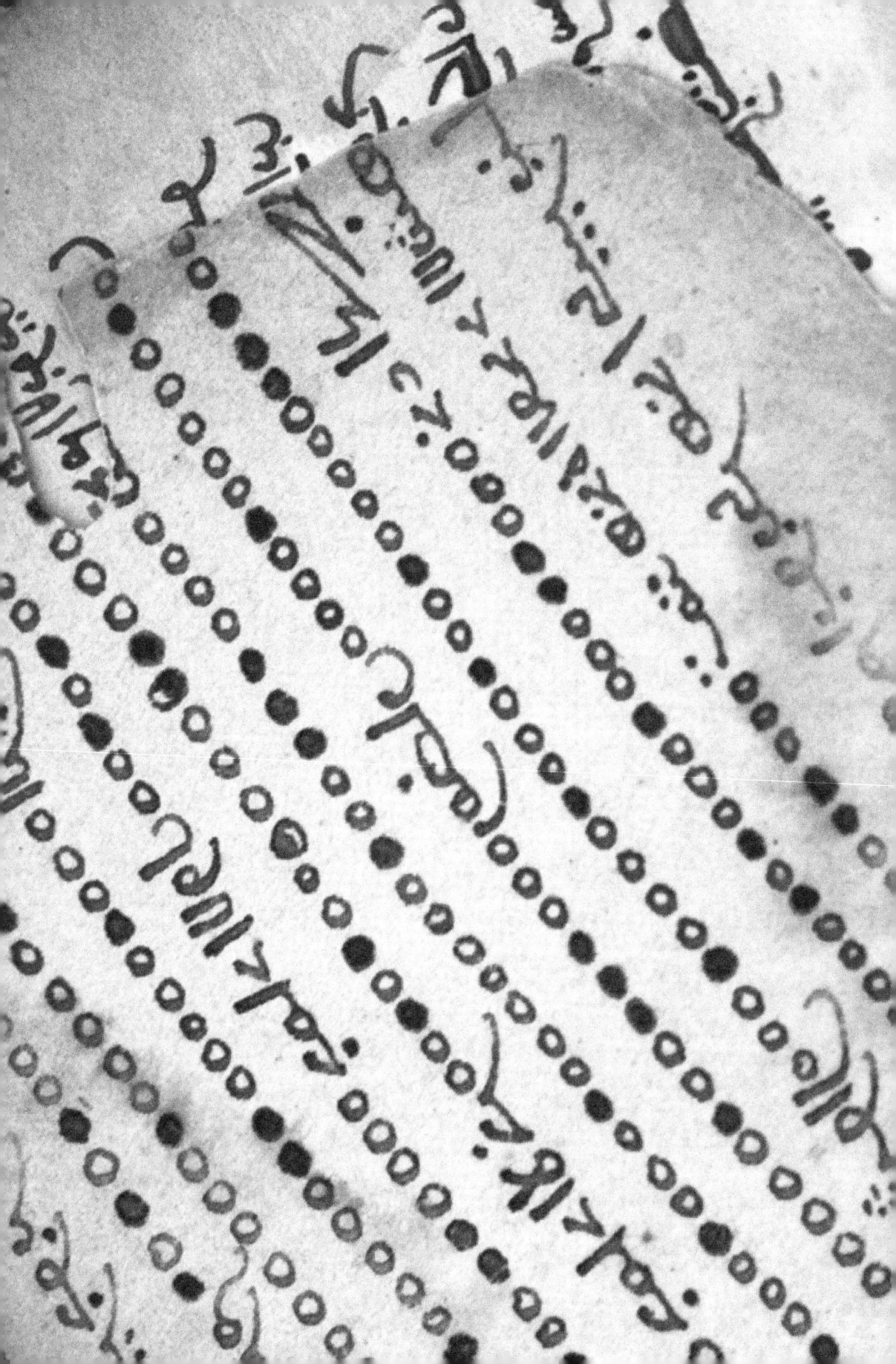

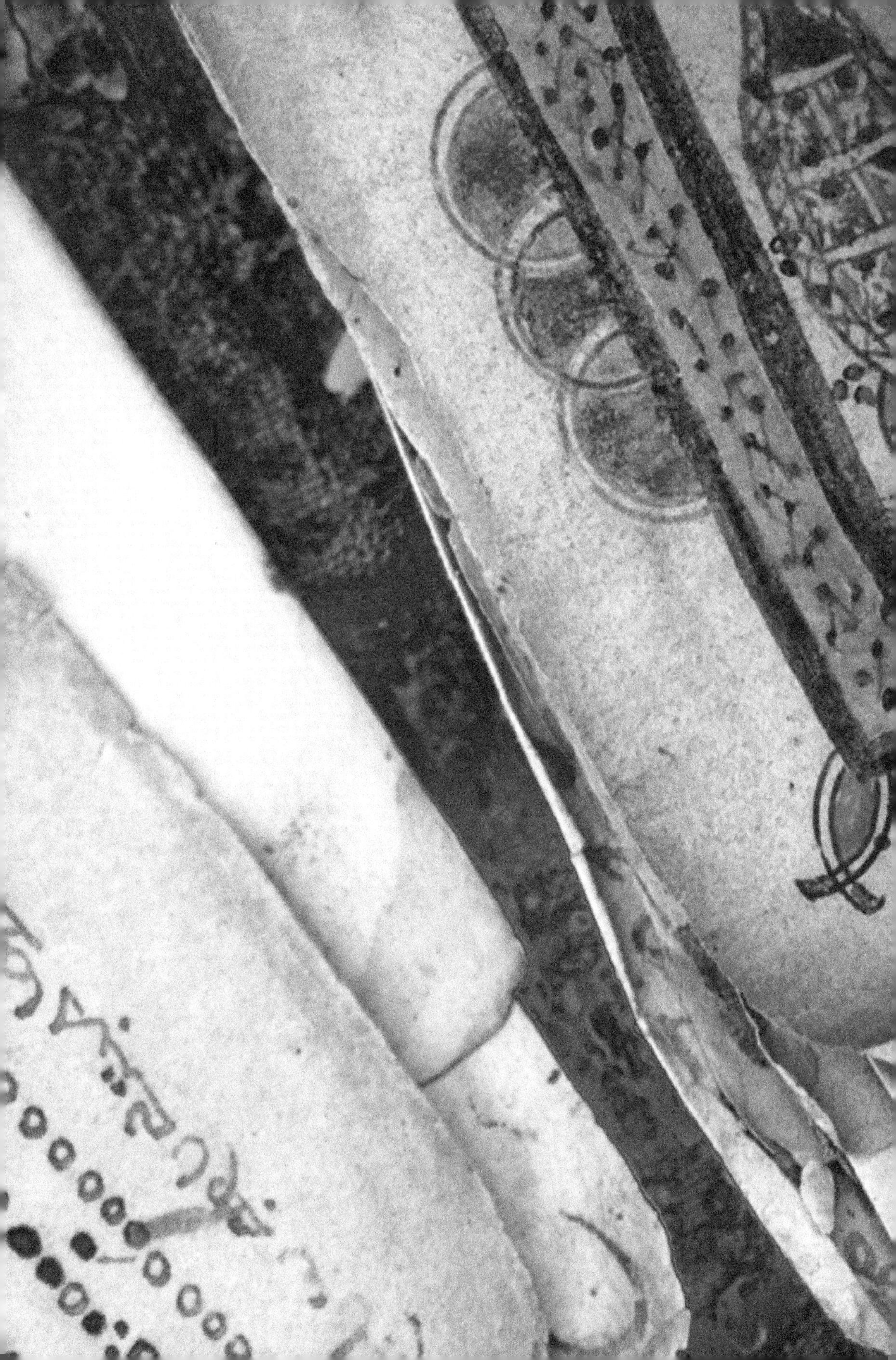

The Mande Charter

By Cheikh Hamidou Kane,
writer

Although there is no longer any question of humankind's African origins, there is still some debate about Africa's place in History, especially Sub-Saharan Africa. Even today, it is said that Africa has no history, that it is burdened with a sickness locating it outside of history, *hic et nunc*. Why is it that this curse does not extend to Africa's northern regions, above all in the northeast where Egypt is located? The most obvious difference between these two halves of the same continent is the presence or absence of writing, a technology that prolongs the word's existence in space and time. In one case, there is copious evidence of writing's long standing existence; in the other, the word simply flies away and therefore seems less trustworthy.

The Occidental Sudanese Sahel is one of the most notorious places on the continent where the word tends to take flight: a land of orality. The griots are the curators of the oral tradition, the servants and guardians who commit themselves to its maintenance and preservation. Separated at vast distances in this land, distributed across Mali, Guinea, Guinea-Bissau, Gambia, and Senegal, there are a half dozen villages that are dedicated to its conservation. These days, thanks to print media, electromagnetism, and computers, writing has, in its turn, grown wings and joined forces with its spoken counterpart. Their union will henceforth always be possible.

In the late 1990s, a meeting took place between a number of griots from villages that are dedicated to the preservation of orality and a wide array of radio outlets in rural West Africa. At this meeting, the universe of the written word, where words are transcribed and transported upon television screens, the guardians of the oral tradition disclosed to the entire world that they had in their possession a founding document of human history, the document known as the *Mande Charter*, which was enacted by the Emperor of Mali, Sundiata Keita in 1236.

Written about the same time as the *Magna Carta*, this text addresses the same basic questions germane to safeguarding the personal security and moral integrity of all humankind, the securing of a space of liberty that the sovereign promises to protect. It also delineates the diverse social categories of those who belong to the body politic, rules governing coexistence between the various ethnic groups, religions, age groups, genders, but also man and his environment.

The griots attest that this charter was not the brainchild of Sundiata. The Emperor merely adopted codes that had existed from time immemorial, from the days of the Ghana Empire and from broader Sudanese-Sahelian societies. He simply collected them and then enacted them into a law governing all those residing in

the Empire from then on.

Timbuktu was one center of this lawful space, a place where the oral tradition intersected with Arab Islamic writing. As a great number of these Arabic language manuscripts confirm, black ink on white paper, Africans from the world of the spoken word attained remarkable degrees of culture, civilization, and history.

On Sound Principles of Governance[1]

Presented and Translated
by Saad Traoré
(School of Advanced Studies and Social Sciences)

The author of this treatise on good governance is Abdul Karim Al Maguly, who was also an advisor to the emperor, the Askiya Muhammad. The author wrote his essay in support of the principles of governance. This work came into being in conditions remarkably similar to those of Nicolas Machiavelli, the founder of political science and international relations, when he wrote *The Prince* on behalf of Laurent de Medici, the Governor of Florence in the 17th century. But, there is one notable difference in their individual circumstances: Machiavelli wrote his book without being asked to do so, presenting it to his sovereign in the guise of a gift. His work, which remains relevant in our own era, was also more widely disseminated than the work of Al-Maguly.

This last point is enormously significant. This has also been the fate of most of these African manuscripts, which have gone unread despite the fact that they contain a vast amount of human knowledge.

The document excerpted here includes a brief introduction and thirty chapters on good governance.

1. *Misbah al-arwah wa mizan al-arbah liman husa bihaqiqati al-salam fi al-kifahi*
« Lanterne (lampe) des âmes et la balance
des bénéfices, particulièrement à celui qui est concerné par la sensibilité de
la paix dans la lutte ».

Manuscrit du XVe siècle, n° 2145, institut Ahmed-Baba.

Introduction:

The contents of this work extend an invitation to the prince or sovereign to avoid the excesses of bad behavior and implore God to uphold him in his belief. It reminds him that rulers are earthly representatives of Allah: they are duty-bound to both spiritual and temporal powers. The virtues of the ruler are legion: because he is the delegate of the prophet, the task that falls to him is quite heavy. For this reason, he should never cease to fear Allah and always bear in mind that death is certain.

First Chapter:

"On Good Faith and Why The Sovereign Must Be Virtuous"

The management of the empire must attend to Allah's peace of mind but without abandoning the desire for power. All sensible and virtuous persons are therefore well advised to flee from positions of power. However, should one find oneself in a position of power, one must always rely upon Allah. Faith in God should govern each and every action of the ruler. Is also imperative to always bear in mind that one is merely the servant of Allah. If you have attained a position of power, it is through the grace of God since many other persons who are more gifted than you could have held the same position. It is therefore essential to place all your fears and hopes in God. Your greatest preoccupation should be securing the benefit and well being of the population you serve. Never forget that God placed you in this position to create a better life for all on His behalf, both in this world and the next.

Second Chapter:

"Why It Is the King's Duty to Always Dress In Royal Garb"

The emperor is obliged to always dress in royal garb. He should anoint himself in perfume, wearing the most finely tailored clothes at all times. He should also adorn himself at all times with magnificent ceremonial relics, compliant with Islamic law. However, it is essential that he avoid outfitting himself in any way that could feminize him. He must also not abuse the public treasury. Hence, he should not adorn himself in gold or silver unless it is incumbent upon him to do so. A ruler should always sit upright and be attentive to his posture. He should shun frivolous mannerisms. He should not make unseemly bodily gestures in public: in the case of yawning, for example, he should always cover his mouth with the back of his hand. The monarch should always think carefully before he speaks: the truth should be his first priority. Only silence is majestic. His voice should be measured. His word is the reflection of his soul, and his soul is what best defines him. There are two types of people he should always avoid: a proud pauper and a wealthy liar. You should therefore speak only the truth and keep all your promises (in opposition to rulers who believe that, "promises are only binding upon those who receive them"). The ruler should set the standard in all circumstances.

The ruler should not tolerate contemptible people in his entourage or at court. This is so because the ruler will be judged by his entourage: by surrounding himself with the best people he will win the confidence of his subjects. Those rulers who surround themselves with advisors of ill repute are always held in low esteem. People are defined according to their associates and the society they keep, as everyone knows. As said in the Occident, "tell me who your friends are, and I will tell you who you are."

Third Chapter:

"On the Necessary Measures to Insure His Government Is Well Organized"

Good government comes from making good political choices. Every political leader should organize his power with all possible contingencies in mind. He should have at his disposal a number of people who are always near at hand: advisors, secretaries, close confidants to manage his affairs, accountants, emissaries, spies, guards on duty both day and for night. He should also surround himself with scholars, sages, judges who are both loyal and fair, and seniors to guide him. His judges should be pious men who labor on God's behalf, ministers who are devoted to Allah, courageous men always on the alert, good doctors to attend to him at all times. In case of war, he must surround himself with ministers who are able to mobilize his soldiers in defense of his territory, war strategists, etc. This is essential because war is a matter of ruse [cf. Clausewitz similarly observes that war is not simply a matter of which of the two powers involved happens to be the strongest; its logic is better defined as the amoral exercise of rationality for purposes of combat].

Fourth Chapter:

"On the Vigilance that the Monarch Must Exercise Both at Home and Abroad"

Leadership presupposes a claim, a demonstration of the ruler's force that is backed up by divine sanction. He must therefore distinguish his family from the source of his power. It also essential that he enlist brave soldiers to hold insects and other vermin (social parasites) at bay. He should associate instead with the greatest of lions (the bravest men in his kingdom). The monarch should inspire fear. Doing so will bring him comfort for his own security and enable him to govern well. Except for those who are closest and most loyal to you, the door should always be shut upon your daily habits, your food preferences, and your private life. Surround yourself only with loyal and obliging friends. Sleep only in secure places. Your personal guard should be composed of strong and loyal men who are highly skilled warriors. Never stop suspecting the motives of others. You must also distrust all those who meddle in affairs that don't concern them.

Fifth Chapter:

"Why it is Useful For the Monarch to Stay Informed on all Current Affairs"

The leader should put questions to those who are informed in order to understand everything that is happening around him. He should attend to the well being of orphans and the disabled. Following the death of one his subjects, he should know who stands to inherit the estate of the deceased as well as the heir's closest relations. It is essential to make inquiries regarding the salaries of public officials, to take an interest in their individual situations and their problems and verify that they are performing their duties, so that the incompetent may be treated accordingly. He should not tolerate people who like to stir up trouble. Public servants who make groundless complaints should be removed from office. Those who harbor evil intentions can do far more damage than the incompetent. All work should be performed in a spirit of good will. Only suitable candidates should be selected to replace those who are removed from office. The ruler should be aware that the relative success of his administration is the direct result of his own actions: he himself will be judged according to the good or evils things that they do.

Sixth Chapter:

"Of the Necessity of Impartiality in the Ruler's Decisions"

Power walks upon the two feet of justice and goodness. Justice entails respecting the rights of each individual. Goodness consists of acting in a manner that is beyond reproach. The impartiality of the sovereign should be manifest whenever he is required to render judgment between two disputing parties: it is necessary to exercise justice when weighing the actions of opposed parties up till the final moment of decision. Even if one of the two parties seeks to reconcile, the ruler must remember that he is their judge, not their friend. Both parties should be granted the same amount of time to present their cases. Fairness demands that only those of sound moral character be allowed to stand as witnesses. ...

Seventh Chapter:

"On the Resources From Where The State Should Draw Its Revenues"

It is of duty of the sovereign to draw revenues on behalf of the State when God authorizes him to do so. Leniency is the heart of power. The basis of leniency and generosity is respect for the private property of others. The longevity of your rule and the brilliance of your power will stem from your respect for private property. On the other hand, an insatiable appetite for riches and lack of respect for private property will surely undermine your rule.

Resources that are divinely sanctioned include *zakkat* (alms giving) of livestock and agricultural foods, the *zakat-al-fitr* (on the morning of the feast of Ramadan), mining resources, one fifth of all booty acquired in times of war, and taxes, etc. The wealth of a deceased person who is without a successor is also a legitimate source of revenue for you, etc. If the monarch is just in financial management, the people have a duty to pay him these fees. The sovereign should avoid provoking his subjects and corrupting his people, for these things are forbidden. Men of law in the king's retinue should not accept bribes, either before or after the fact. Gifts from plaintiffs should never be accepted.

Eighth Chapter:

"The Sectors Where Collected Treasury Funds Must Be Invested"

Public funds authorized for deposit should be dispensed only in those sectors that God deems legitimate. Generosity will secure the ruler's longevity and power. On the other hand, greed and excessive spending will bring him harm. The generous acts of a sovereign may include making necessary expenditures at any time they are truly necessary, according to the means available to him. To do more than this is contrary to the rules of power management. The Holy Quran provides precise instructions regarding the investment of public funds, and the ruler should know what they are. They include expenditures on charity for the poor, necessities, public employees, those who rack up debts in the service of Allah, travelers in distress, etc.

Description on Page 80 of image on Page 81] A poem by Ibn Asim entitled *Tufat al-hukkam fi nukati al-uqud wal-Ahkam*. Its theme is a treatise on law. The verses presented here address to topic of inheritance rights.

عدة أبياتها تعددا ... هل تشفعا في الآن أبدا

وقصد توجيه هنا انتهى ... والحمد لله بغير منتهى

ثم الصلاة ختمه كما ابتدا ... على الرسول المصطفى محمد

وآله وصحبه الأخيار ... ما كور الليل على النهار

كملت الأرجوزة المرسومة بتحفة
الحكام في نكت العقود والأحكام
بحمد الله وحسن عونه
اللهم اغفر لمالكه وكاتبه
ولقاريه آمين
... آمين

صاحب
هذا الكتاب
...
صاحب هذ...

وصلوات ربنا على المختار
صلاة دائمة بدوام الأبد
على يد مذنب فقير
محمد أبو محمد زاغوي
سألتك بأخا المضار
والوالدين والإخوان
ثم الأحياء والأموات من المسلمين
اللهم يا عظيم ... منه

وعلى آله وصحبه الأبرار
ما غنت الحمام على الغصن
إلى رحمة ربه عبد ربه
المغربي المالكي الأشعري
أرجو لكاتب القلب بالغفران
بحرمة الدبور الفرح
وكل واحد وقال آمين
وهب لطالبه الجنة

[redacted]

... هذا الكتاب
...

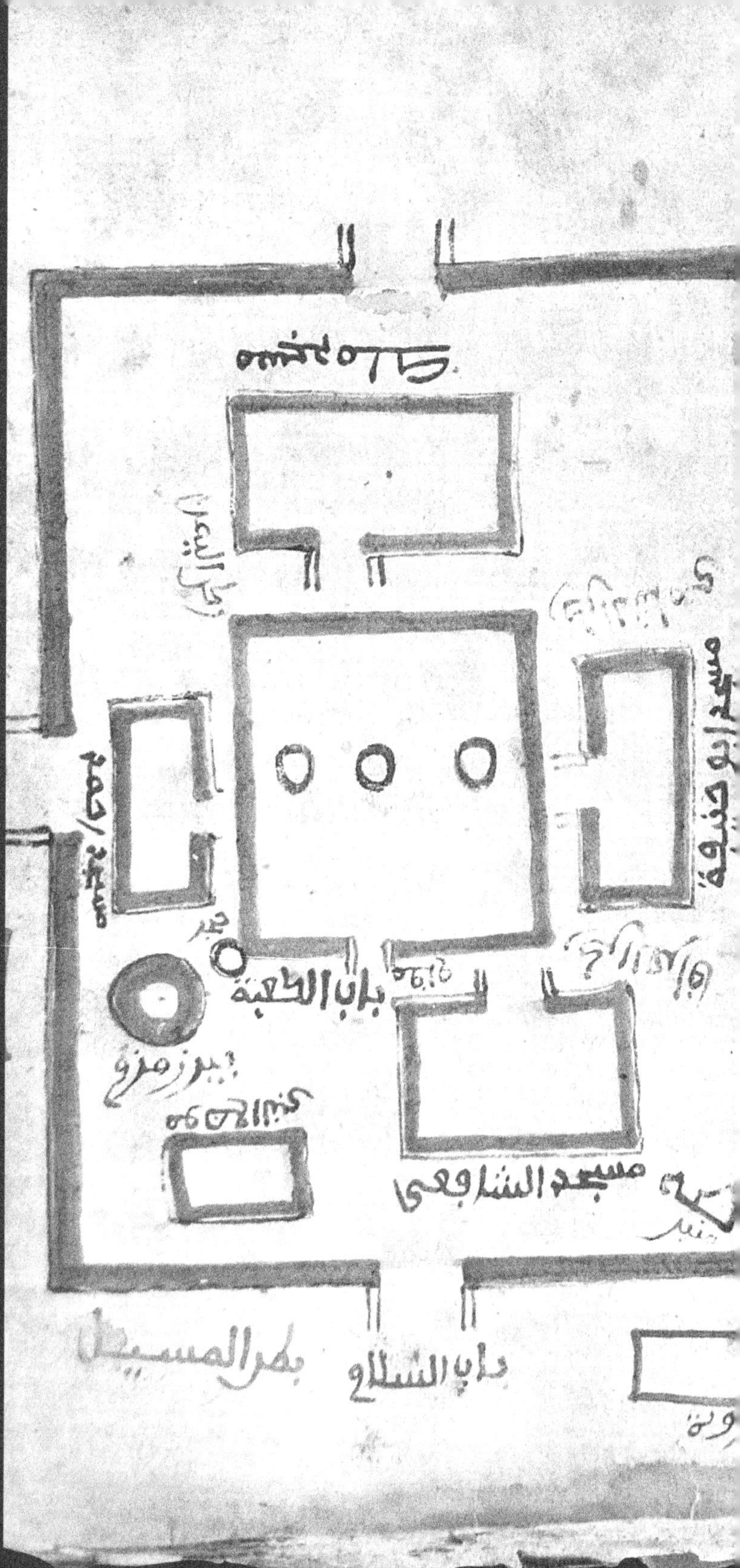

Left page: A manuscript depicting an overview of Mecca.

Right page: An overview of the tomb of the Prophet at Medina alongside the tombs of the first two caliphs (Abu Bakr and Umar).

صاحب هذه الدلائل
أحمد بن
رحمه الله
ولجميع المسلمين

The Property Question

Raising the question of land and its ownership provides yet more evidence of the highly developed nature of Songhay civilization. While in Europe it was unheard of that a sovereign might bestow land (as well as cattle) upon his subjects. Yet, the Askiyas did so in written decrees whenever the merits of the beneficiaries justified such an act.

The *Tarikh al fattash*, as discussed by Michal Tymowski at an academic colloquium in Rabbat in 2009, documents how the Askiya Muhammad gave a gift to the sons of the *ulema* Mori Hawgaru in 1508. During the reign of the dynasty of Sunni Ali Ber, the children of Mori Hawgaru were persecuted because they were orthodox Muslims. At that time, Mori Hawgaru's children were put in irons and deported to an island at a tributary of the Niger. They later complained about their treatment. As a form of compensation, the Askiya gave them one hundred cows and ten slaves. But the brothers of those who were given this gift saw things differently. They came as a group before the Askiya and asked him to reverse his judgment, which he did.

Their quarrel was not simply about the amount and type of goods given, but the very notion of ownership itself. At this time, a tacit conflict had developed over the role of Islam in the social structure of the Empire's methods of production. The question of ownership was at the center of this conflict. Should ownership be collective or private? By giving the children of the *ulema* private property that belonged to them alone and not the entire family, the Askiya had effectively cast his support on behalf of those in favor of private ownership. The "modern" idea of private property in the Songhay Empire had already taken root in Africa.

A S. M. Cissoko remarked in 1890, the maturity attained by this Empire has been underestimated for far too long. In fact, no one living in either Cairo or Rome fathomed the degree to which "the Sudanese genius had been able to Africanize Islam."[1]

1. *Historie de l'Afrique occidentale*, Présence africaine, 1966.

A manuscript on astronomy depicting the circles of the Zodiac. The goal was to predict the future through combining the numbers and letters.

عابر حنا وحار [illegible] اذا حرويا حارة [illegible] ما استعمل [illegible] تكتب في الحيوان موضع
[illegible] ثم تكتب على راسه
القلب اسم [illegible] الذي اردت
[illegible] الاعماله
ثلثها من
الرطوبة
[illegible]
[illegible] اذا
[illegible] وسطها
[illegible]

التشريعة المركبة
الحرارة وثلثها
وسد [illegible]
وسد سهل
كان امرا
والابا لحار البا
مزجنا [illegible]
[illegible] المركبة

بسر [illegible] وابد
من الرطوبة مثل الا
ثلثها من الر
طوبة وثلثها
من الحرارة
وثلثها
باردة
يابسة
وهذه
الدواير

هي اصل الا
عمال ليتصرف
في كل صنف منها
ما يوافقه في العمل صفة:
ما يعمل في وضع وبوعه في عمه زيادة ما في بالحنه بعد عدله وجمله
ما ضلعه بعد كله تنزيد عليه [illegible] وتنقص بوه سبطا والخيرات
غزد فيه بوه شرحه انك تستعبر الوفق مثاله كا

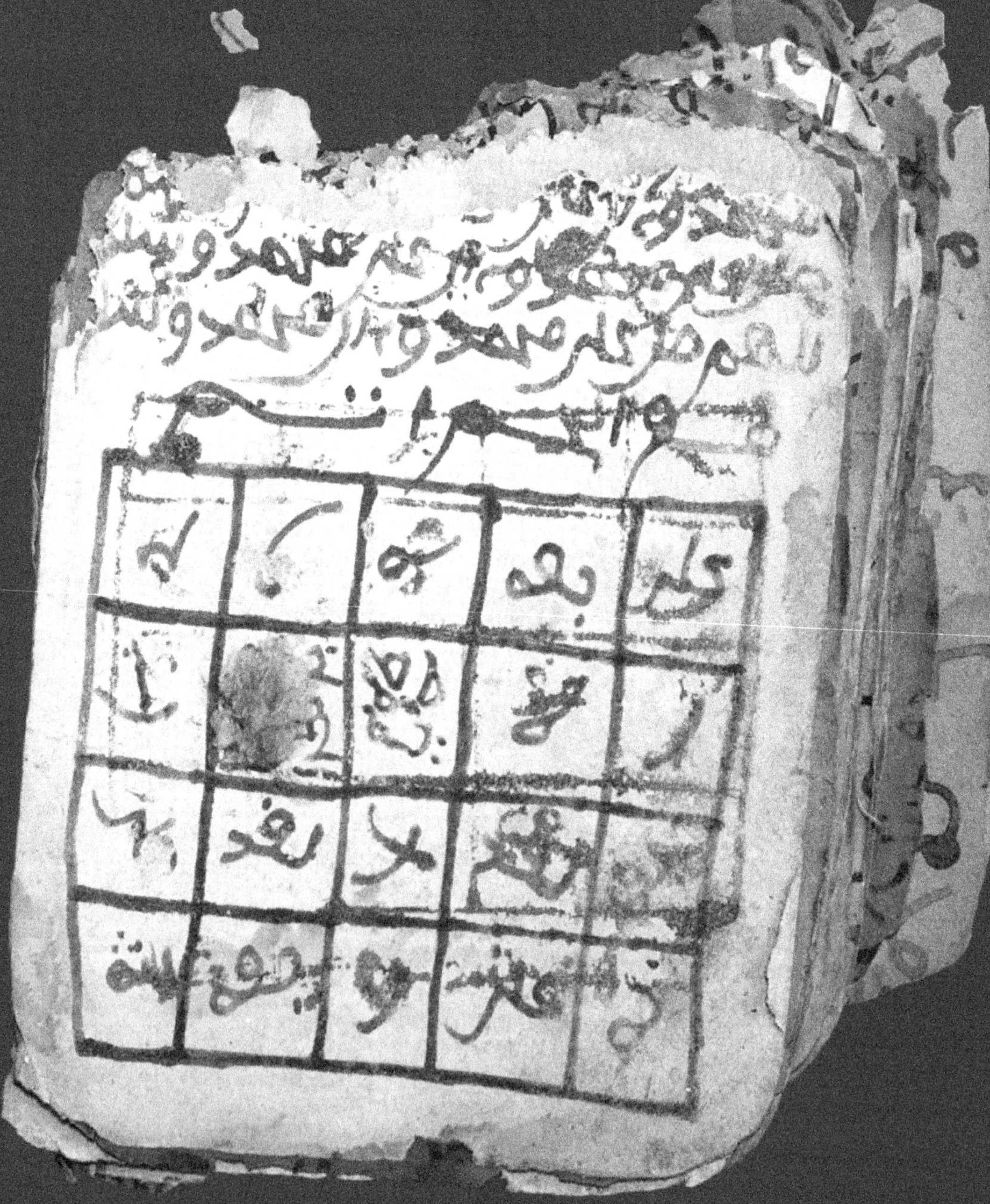

A magic square for the art of divination (with the use of dice, pebbles...)

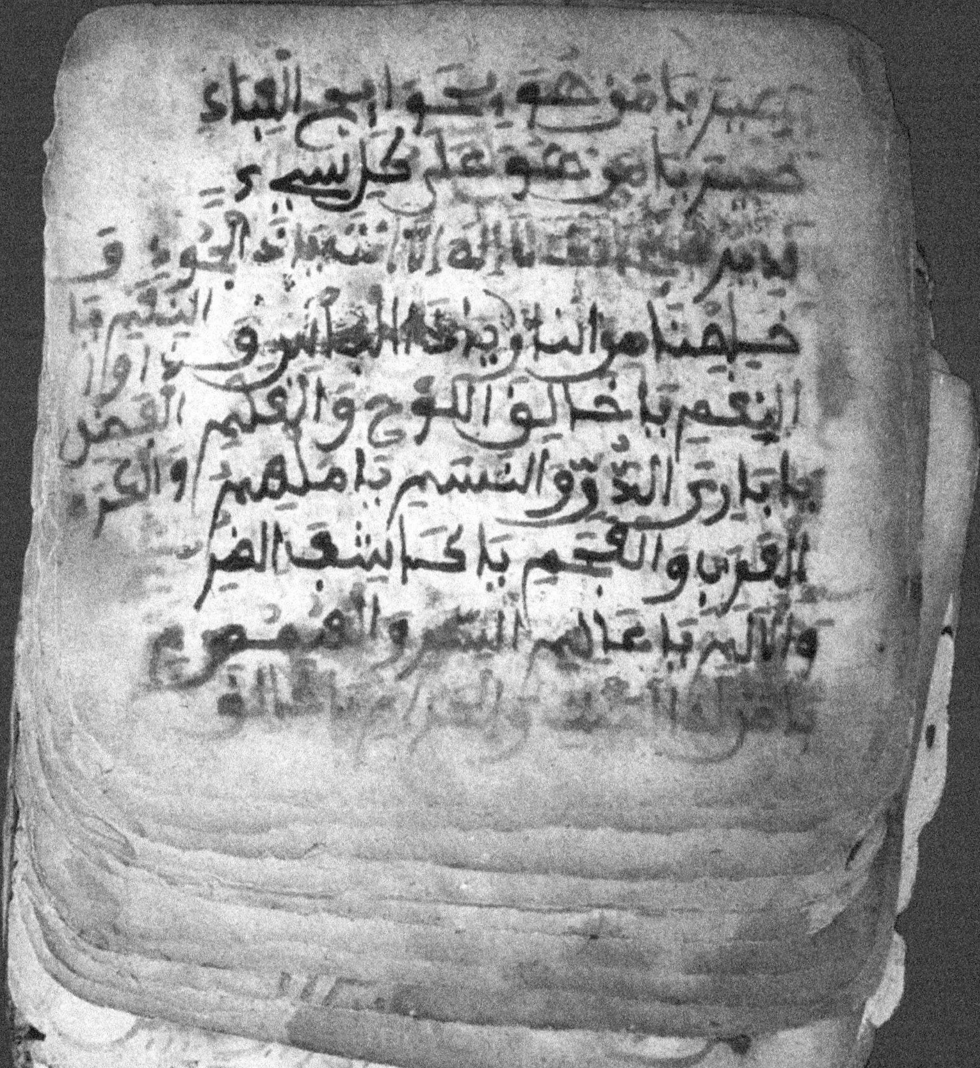

The page of a manuscript with divine incantations.

Medicine

In the domain of medicine, discoveries made in manuscripts dating back to the second part of the 14th century reveal the degree to which the healing arts were akin to modern surgery practices.1

We are told that a certain Ibn Hayttham wrote a document that describes a form of cataract surgery, based upon methods inspired by the ophthalmologist Alghafaki of Cordoba in the 12th century. We also learn that, from the 8th century on, the use of plants in treating tropical illnesses was commonplace.

What is less well known is that local medical practices had even won renown for some of its practitioners. This was the case with a certain Aben Ali, a doctor who was trained at Timbuktu's University of Sankore. Later, he relocated to be close to his master Ysalguier who lived in Gao; however, Ysalguier was originally from the French city of Toulouse, a city he would return to at the end of his life. He relocated there in 1419 and made history when, in barely five days, he was able to save the future Charles VII from yellow fever after the king's doctors had declared him to be beyond hope.

Two later publications, *Les Annales de Toulouse*, which appeared in 1687, as well as an article in *Essais de literature pour la connaissance des livres*, dated 1702, document this historical event.

1. Cited in *Recueil de sources arabes concernant l'Afrique occidentale* du VIII siècle au XVI siècle, translated and annotated by Joseph Cuoq, CNRS, 1985.

وكان يتهمها على الزنى ودخول الرجال عليها قاله في كتاب
المعجمة و من اخذ خصيتي الديك وجففها وسحقها
وخلط برماده ذكره وجامع امراته فانه لا يقدر احد ان
يطاها غيره باذن الله او كتبت في راس القلم اي الذكر
يجامع امراته وهذا ما يكتب فاض باغ عاج قال بعض
المراد بالقلم راس الحشفة قاله السيوطي و من اخذ دم
دجاجة سوداء عند ذبحها وخالطه مع العسل ويجعل
شيئا على راس ذكره ويجامع به زوجته فان المراة تجد
لذة عظيمة تكاد ان تخرج عقلها لشدة الجماع وصابة
شدة الذي وكذلك اذا طليت باحليلك بمرارة دجا
جة عند الجماع وكذلك اذا قرات قوله تعالى امراة نوح
وامراة لوط كانتا تحت عبدين من عبادنا كالحيض
عند الاضطجاع وارادة الجماع تجد لذة عظيمة مجرب
صحيح قاله في كتاب المعجمة ومن اخذ مرارة الـ
دجاجة ويلطخ بها احليله عند الجماع فانه يهيج الباءة

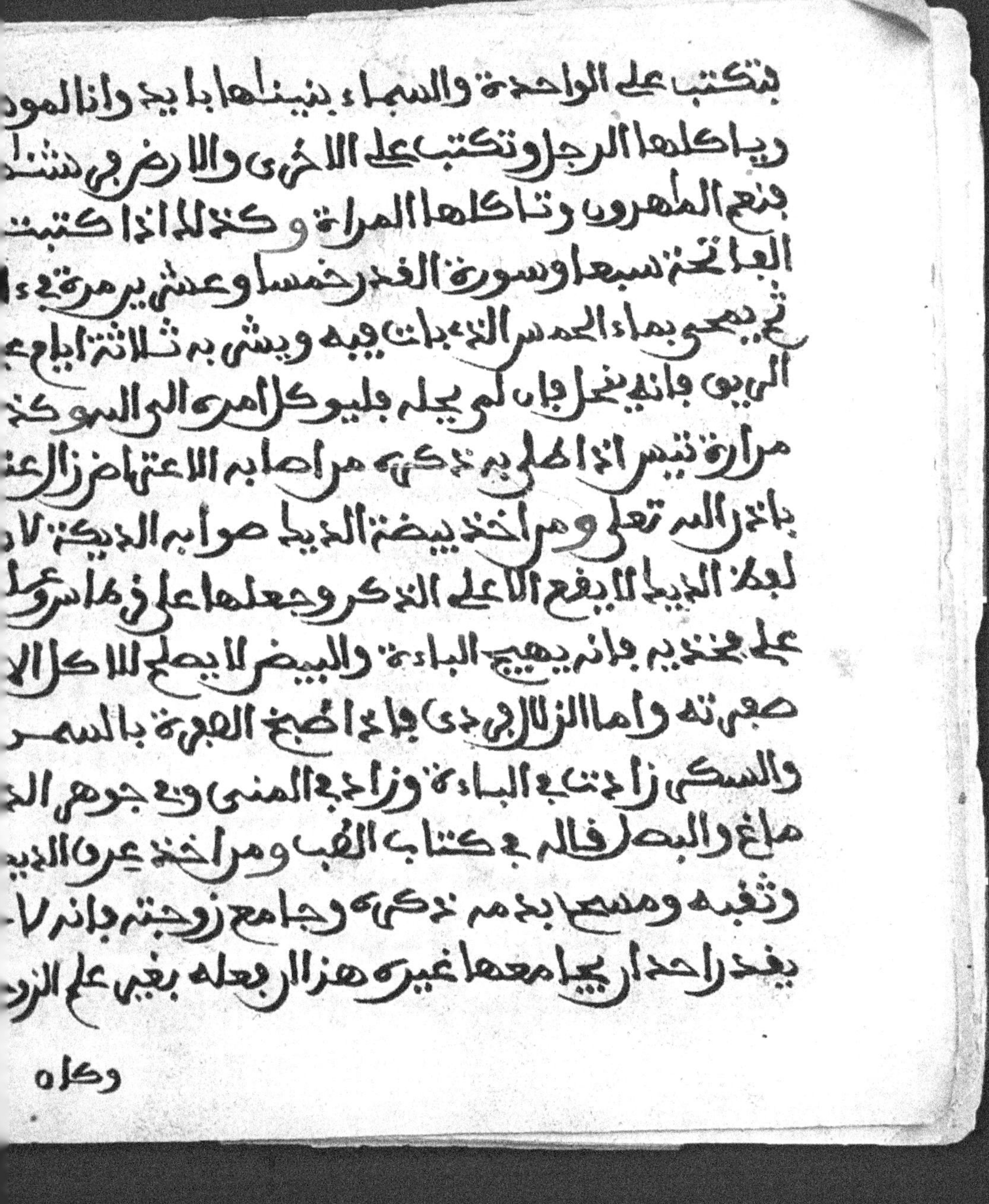
بتكتب على الواحدة والسماء بنيناها بايد وانا المو
ويا كلها الرجل وتكتب على الاخرى والارض فرشنا
فنعم الماهدون وتاكلها المراة وكذلك اذا كتبت
الفاتحة سبعا وسورة القدر خمسا وعشرين مرة في
ثم يمحو بماء الحمص الذبابات فيه ويشرب به ثلاثة ايام في
الريق فانه يفحل فان لم يجده فليوكل امره الى السو ك
مرارة تيس اذا اطلى به ذكره من اصابه الاعتراض زال عنه
باذن الله تعالى ومن اخذ بيضة الديك صواب الديكة لا
لبطن الديك لا يبقى الا على الذكر وجعلها على ذماس و
على فخذيه فانه يهيج الباءة والبيض لا يصلح الا اكل الا
صفرته واما الزلال فيردي فاذا اصبح الصفرة بالسمن
والسكر زاد في الباءة وزاد في المني وفي جوهر الد
ماغ والبصل قاله في كتاب الطب ومن اخذ عرق الديك
وثقبه ومسح به ذكره وجامع زوجته فانه لا
يقدر احد ان يجامعها غيره هذا ان فعله بغير علم الزو
وكره

Advice for successful copulation and for keeping one's spouse from the temptations of infidelity. The above excerpt is a recipe that consists of testicles or chicken blood to achieve these results.

The Treatment of Illnesses, Internal and External[1]

Theme: Traditional Medicine

This manuscript, which is more than three hundred pages in length, is organized into five sections:

INTRODUCTION:

The author demonstrates the importance of health, the essential ingredient for success in all physical or intellectual activities.

FIRST CHAPTER:

This chapter focuses on the mystical treatment of illnesses with the use of certain Quranic verses and invocations.

SECOND CHAPTER:

In this chapter, the author discusses the use of animal organs or their derivatives in healing certain illnesses.

THIRD CHAPTER:

This chapter addresses the use of plants for treating illnesses.

FOURTH CHAPTER:

This chapter addresses the use of minerals, rocks, and water that contain medicinal properties.

1. Manuscript Number 1045; 5719. Ahmad Baba Institute. Author: Shaykh Sidi Ahmad Ibn Umar Arraqadi Alkunti (deceased in 1592-93 at Timbuktu).

The cover of a manuscript from the 17th century, found in an iron canister at Segu but originally from Timbuktu. Couverture d'un manuscrit du xviie siècle trouvé

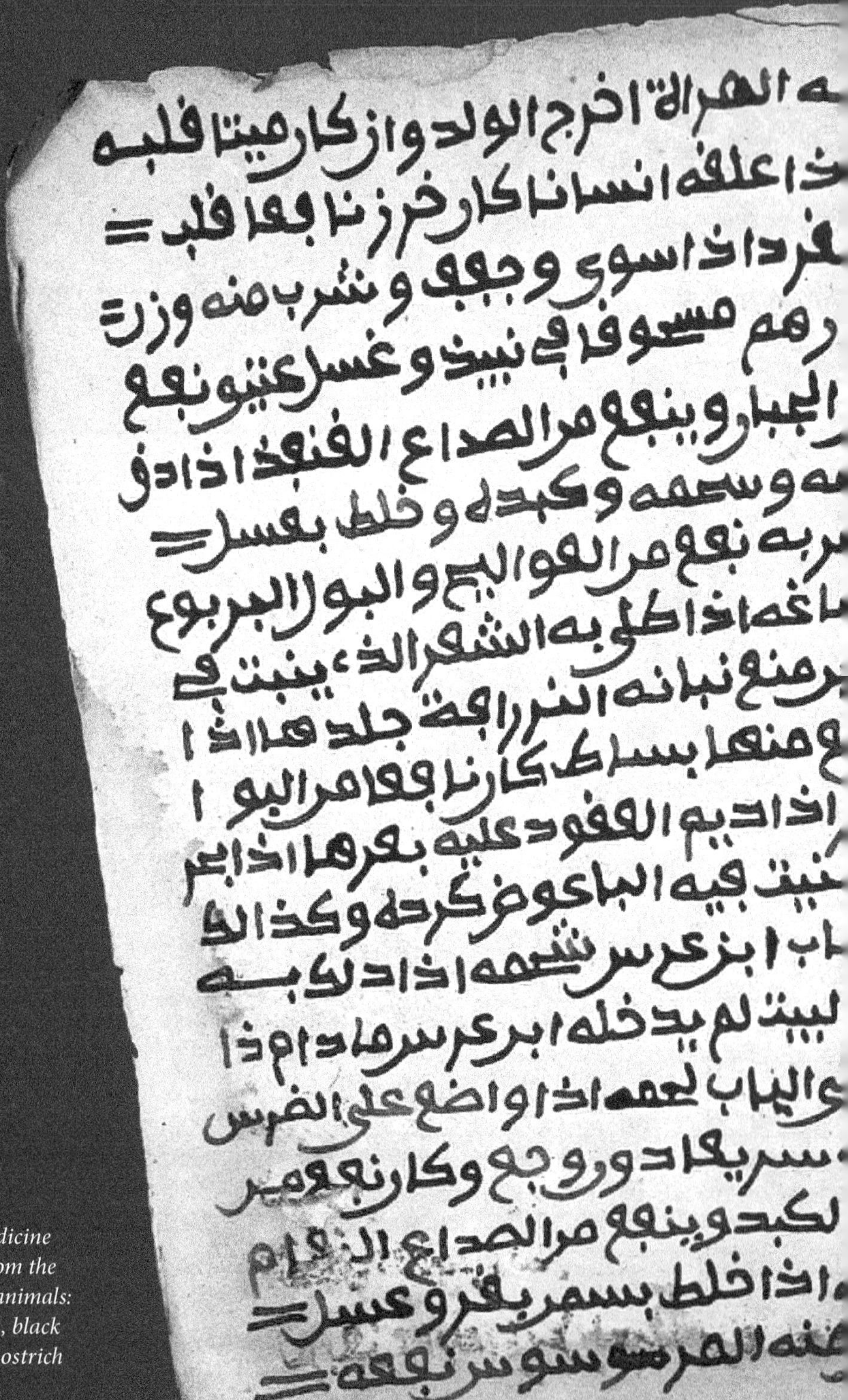

A treatise on medicine with remedies from the meat of various animals: monkeys, hyenas, black dogs, hedgehogs, ostrich eggs, weasels...

من النمر ومرارته سم قاتل الضبع راسه
اذا وضع في برج الحمام كثر فيه الطير جلد
ه اذا امسكه الانسان على عضده لم ينبح
عليه كلب راس ذيب اذا علق في بروج
حمام لم يقربه سنانير كلبه اذا علق
على راس رمح واجتمعت اليه جماعة بالر
مح يريدون لم يصلون اليه مادام الكلب
معلقا على رمح الكلب نابه اذا علق على
صبي خرجت السنانه بلا الم كبده اذا شو
ي واكله على عضة برا من ساعته شحم
الكلب اذا طلي على الخنازير نفعها عين
الكلبة الاسود اذا دفنت في دار خربت
تلك الدار لبرهة وسقط اذن الكلبة
اذا لوثت به فتيلة وسقت بين اقوا م
دبرا بعضهم بعض كارو وسهم روس
التيس الثعلب [illegible] ابه اذا علق على صبي يفزع
لم يفزع ابدا وبر السنور الاسود اذا بخر
به

Translation of an excerpt in verse from

The Book on Healing External and Internal Illnesses That Plague the Body[1]

Presentation and Translation by
Floréal Sanagustin
(University of Lyon and ENS, ICAR Laboratory)

The peculiarity of this manuscript, besides its considerable length (503 pages), is it blending of medical and magical practices, its dual reliance upon scientific traditions and popular ones. Its historical value resides in the fact that it enables us to gage the state of medical knowledge in Sub-Saharan regions at a relatively late date, the 17th century. It is clear that the foundations of Arab-Muslim science were established in these regions from the moment they were Islamized. The religious sciences were taught throughout the region at the same time as the rational sciences, especially in centers of learning such as Timbuktu. To this day, tens of thousands of Arabic manuscripts in this city provide evidence of local scientific activities, as also documented in the work of VECMAS (the program for the "Development, Editing, and Criticism of Sub-Saharan Manuscripts in Arabic").

The author of this work is the Shaykh Sid Ahmad Ibn Umar Al Raqqadi Al Kunti. He came from a branch of the Kunta and was a descendent of Sidi Umar, the grand master of the Qadriyya of the Tekrur and the Sahara, who died in 960/1552 (Muslim calendar/Christian calendar). Our author, a descendant of the former, is referred to in some places by the name of Sidi Ahmad Al Khalifa. He was also known to be a very learned scholar and a renowned Sufi shaykh, who was considered to be a bulwark of Islam (*qutb*). He played an important role in establishing the religious prestige of the Kunta family at the heart of the Qadiriyya in Azawad (a region to the north of Timbuktu). Shortly before his death, he immigrated to Timbuktu where he became the first Kunta to wield considerable influence. He did so

1. Cf. F. Sanagustin, *Livre de la guérison des maladies externs et internes affectant les corps*, by Shaykh Ahmad Al Raqqadi Al Kunti, edition critique, ENS Édition, Lyon, 2010-2011. Manuscript 116 from the Mamma Haidara Library of Timbuktu.

to insure that his descendants might always occupy an important place in this town. He is buried to the east of Timbuktu where his tomb still stands. In fact, many pilgrims visit his tomb on Thursday morning of each week.

In the portion of the manuscript that the author devotes to sexual relations, he includes a long poem that is attributed to Shaykh Tedghi. This poem, which is translated below, discusses the benefits of sexual intercourse, but also its risks, by clarifying the best times for the venereal act and the most suitable positions the lovers should adopt. The fact that the esteemed Sufi deems it suitable to write a didactic poem on sexual relations is not rare in classic Arab-Muslim civilization, where most works on the topic of love are infused with erotic sentiments (*Kutub al-bah*). They too were written by doctors and theologians.[2]

Partial Translation of the Poem

The abuse of coitus is injurious to those who suffer from an excess of bile or melancholy. When one is phlegmatic and sluggish of blood, even if one feels predisposed towards the venereal act, it is preferable to limit one's sexual relations to no more than three times a week, spaced out in a timely fashion. One should not copulate two separate times in the same day or the same night, which could prove fatal. Above all, one should not excessively ejaculate, for sperm is the main substance of blood and the resource of the spirit. Those who abuse coitus to excess will soon languish. They will experience a loss of power as well as the loss of hair pigmentation. Here is a poem on coitus written by Shaykh Al Tadghi,[3] may his soul be granted peace:

Be aware that the abuse of coitus
weakens the body, especially
hearing.

There is no doubt that it causes
illnesses through depleting
one's vital forces and
engendering migraines.

It is also the source of lumbago,
weakness in the kidneys, and
no doubt the loss of sexual
appetite.

During summer and spring,
coitus is much to be desired,
less so in autumn and winter.

And the more you honor old
women, the less you will
appreciate the young,

The opposite holds true for
women. Good men, with
God's help, hold fast to these
precepts!

Its Benefits

It is common knowledge that
to abstain from sex causes
migraines and delirium.

It is proven that doing so causes
heart palpitations, frigid
temperaments, and gout.

It blinds the heart. Do not doubt

2. Cf. *The Delights of the Heart*, by Shaykh Tifashi (650/1253) and *The Perfumed Garden*, by Shaykh Nafzawi, Tunisian author of the 15th century.

3.Ahmad Ibn Salah Al Tadghi was a Malikite jurist from the Maghreb, who died in 1019/1610. Among other works, he was the author of an erotic work that is probably taken from the title of this poem: *Urjuza tuhfat al-falah fi adab al-jima wal-nikah*. I am grateful to my colleague Abderrahim Saguer (ICAR-ENS of Lyon) for the help that he provided me in the translation of some of these verses.

these words but instead put them into action. If you do so, you will succeed in all your endeavors.

Among its benefits, you should know that it calms anger and often leads to the dissipation of worries and anxiety.

In the same manner, copulating dissipates melancholy. Everyone knows this.

It is commonly said that sexual desire chases away misfortune.

At first, it hardens the heart, but it softens the heart once the act is completed.

The Moments of Coitus

The moment is conducive when she paints her face, anoints herself in perfume, or dresses up.

Be aware that she has invited you at these times and assuredly wants you to cohabit with her.

Make love according to these rules, after her blood flow has ceased and she is pure.

Above all, those who wish to procreate should keep this mind. Do not forget it!

Coitus is enjoyable at the end of the evening, for one feels lighter then. This is a proven fact.

It is also enjoyable at twilight but not before digestion. Do not debate it!

Young folks! You should know that the heroes of old sometimes gazed upon the face of those whom they loved.

But they also said that doing so is liable to blind the heart, engender contempt, and annihilate love.

Do not caress the vulva with the right hand and always murmur in her ear without thinking.

Above all, know that God protects you during coitus and withdrawal from it.

Begin with banter and sweet words, then embrace her promptly.

Avoid kissing her eyes. Do not have coitus if you have no desire for it. Do not give in to hypocrisy!

My friend, if you caress her well, you will obtain your heart's desires [...]

Helpful Remarks

Before you enter the bedroom, respectfully take off your sandals.

Then, dear friend, squat down and wash your feet with fresh water.

Then sprinkle water in the room, on the door of the house, the walls, and in all nooks and crannies.

If you do so, know that you will relieve this dwelling of its distress.

Also, beneficial and divine blessings will overflow upon it.

Then put your hand on your head and recite the surah *al-A'raf*[4] in its entirety.

When you reach the verse of the Throne,[5] you must invoke God.

"God, please be with us, give us success, bestow upon us the blessings that are permitted to us. Forgive us

And grant to us a child who will be intelligent, obedient, virtuous, loving, and serviceable."

Then pray abundantly and salute the Prophet, who was a good man, and His Family.

Then, without losing any time, do what you must do without thinking too deeply about it.

Tell no one your secrets nor ever speak of the sweetness of this woman. To do so is contemptible.

Do not withdraw from her without first excusing yourself. Should this happen, do not speak of it later.

And if you want her to love you, my friend, put your hand on the back of her head

And say seven times in an exalted voice, "My Friend, God is so close to us[6]..."

And the surah Joseph[7]

And, if you wish to win her heart, at the moment of penetration recite for her,

The surah of the Morning,[8] unencumbered with verbiage, and the surah of the Victory[9] minus two verses.

And if you believe you are the victim of an evil spell, write the surah the Opening[10]; do not forget this!

Write it seven times in a row. As well as this edifying poem. Learn these things!

And (write) the surah *al-Qadr*[11] in its entirety twenty five times. Respect this order!

Write it on a wine jar; then erase the ink with some a slight amount of chickpea water.

Drink it for three days in a row to remove the curse. Remember this lesson!

4. This refers to surah 7.

5. Verse 255 of the *surah al-Baqara*.

6. The conclusion of an unreadable verse.

7. This refers to surah 12 of the Quran. The second caesura is incomprehensible.

8. Surah 93.

9. Surah 110.

10. Surah 1.

11. Surah 97.

A manuscript on rhetoric: enunciation / performatives, truth / falsehoods. The commentary clarifies the sacred character of these questions and offers a definition of religious faith.

منه عنه نسي حتى يمم او كراهة

والغيبانة عرم حيفما ص

جمعة مر المخالفة لما حدله واوصى به ولا تشكار مو لفاجو عزوجل

ذالذنوب التي التوبة

لازب عنها

حدو لقبيده حد المكلبين حدود وامر تقع واوصاهم الا تتعدوا حدوده حدلنا سبحانه الواجب والمندوب والمباح ونفعا نار ب تتعدانا الى فعل المحرم والمكروه من الافعال واوجبنا ناجل وعلى بتقواه وبالفرار من غضبه وعقابه الى الزجر كا عنه وما جعله جل وعلا بفضله امارة على رضاه ونعيمه وثوابه جمع وفقه الله للهناء فظنة علو صيته وجعله جل وعلا بفضله من هنا الجنة كرامينا شرح

الحمد لله رب العلمين والصلاة والسلام على من لا نبي بعده اللهم اغفر لنا ولجميع المسلمين والمسلمات والمومنين والمومنات الاحياء منهم والاموات ووافق الفراغ منه وقت الزوال من يوم الجمعة بلدة ... اللهم اغفر لكاتبه ولوالديه ولجميع المسلمين امين

اسم صاحب هذا الكتاب احمد بن ... عماده بن شاده بن محمد ... ملي

The Power of the Scholars

At the apex of the Songhay Empire in Timbuktu, the teaching of books prospered. For nearly two centuries, knowledge was worth as much as gold in the market place. Students came from Egypt, Andalusia, Morocco, or the Empire of Benin to participate in its great academic traditions by attending the University of Sankore or taking courses at the madrasa in grammar, poetry, and mathematics.

Because the Askiya Muhammad set the standard by involving his men of letters in the affairs of his *Sunna* (or "Court"), foreign doctors from Tichit, Takkeda, or Jenne naturally began to relocate to Timbuktu (such as the Baghayogho brothers, who were renowned scholars, or the Sharif al-Saqalli, who came from Mecca).

All these scholars were nurtured in the teachings of Al Azhar University at Cairo. They were especially steeped in the teaching of the encyclopedic and erudite Al Suyuti,[1] a scholar who is forgotten today, but who nonetheless published five hundred and sixty-one scientific works on matters of law, grammar, linguistics, and Quranic exegesis.

But it did not take long for the scholars of Timbuktu to began debating the theses of these elder scholars and challenge what they found in their commentaries. They did so at the instigation of their master Ahmad Baba. In this way, the City of 333 Saints gradually came to be intellectually emancipated. A quite liberal form of university education took root.

"The teacher's freedom was total," Professor Sékéné Mody Cissoko observes.[2] "All those who held licensed diplomas (*id jajat*) were eligible to teach or work at a school. There was, however, a great difference between the masters of the Quranic school and the most highly esteemed doctors. Still, both wore a big boubou over a long-sleeved shirt and a white turban. They also carried a long staff with a pointed tip in their right hand." At the height of its glory in the 15th century, the town hosted more than twenty-five thousand students who paid their teachers in direct proportion to their "market" ratings. Copyists were paid in gold that was measured by the gram, and the manuscripts themselves were veritable keys that opened the doors to the most prestigious administrative and religious posts.

1.The most prolific Egyptian writer during the era of the Mamelukes, if not Arabic literature in general." *Encyclopédie de L'islam.*

2. Author of *Tombouctou et l'Empire Songhai.* L'Harmattan, 1996..

Libraries were opened everywhere in order to classify the great volume of texts written upon paper from the Far East, the scapula of camels, or sheep-skin.

A random glance at these manuscripts might turn up any of the following:

pharmacopeia handbooks (there is a Sudanese manuscript, number 1224, that discusses of the evils of tobacco; it was written in 1835).

medical treatises (the great Persian scholar Avicenna wrote manuscript number 2309. It addresses the treatments of contagious maladies, broken bones, and dental hygiene in an encyclopedic manner).

treatises on optics (manuscript number 3666 focuses on differences between seeing at daytime and night; it dates from the 11th century),

treatises on astronomy (manuscript number 4058 discusses the earth's dimensions from the position of the stars).

In these libraries, there are also texts with advice on sexual relations between couples (manuscript number 5292, written in the 19th century), and handbooks of grammar and mathematics. By chance, we learn from an imprint on the colophon (the last page of a papyrus manuscript reserved for making notes) that a copyist finished his work two years after an earthquake at Timbuktu. In fact, he notes the seismic aftershocks that were felt after the great Lisbon earthquake...

The most salient characteristic of the Sudanese intellectual tradition was its close link to the rest of the Muslim world. This is the constant that provided the impetus behind Timbuktu's manuscript culture. Evidence for this can be found throughout the Maghreb, Andalusia, and West Africa. Manuals of *figh* (law), logic, or grammar were widely circulated in all of these places. They were copied, annotated with comments, and then put into direct circulation. They form the matrix of an African imagination that more or less held together the various religions, ethnic groups, empires, nomadic and sedentary peoples, and the northern and southern Sahel.

It was Sufism's community oriented spirituality (specifically, that of the Qadriyya) that nurtured this imaginative universe. The Timbuktu scholar Ahmad Baba was the most glorious incarnation of this form of mysticism. He was a leader who set the standard for the Malikite. Along with his elder Muhammad Baghayogho, he was an inspirational figure for all other scholars. The two of them were scholars who never subordinated themselves to the power of the court. They were above all such suspicions. The rulers of the Songhay, including Sunni Ali Ber, who ruled before the Askiya Muhammad, and then the Askiya Dawad and his successors, sometimes became infuriated due to their opposition. As authentic checks upon sovereign power, they were feared because of their readiness to adopt a haughty public demeanor on behalf of Islam.

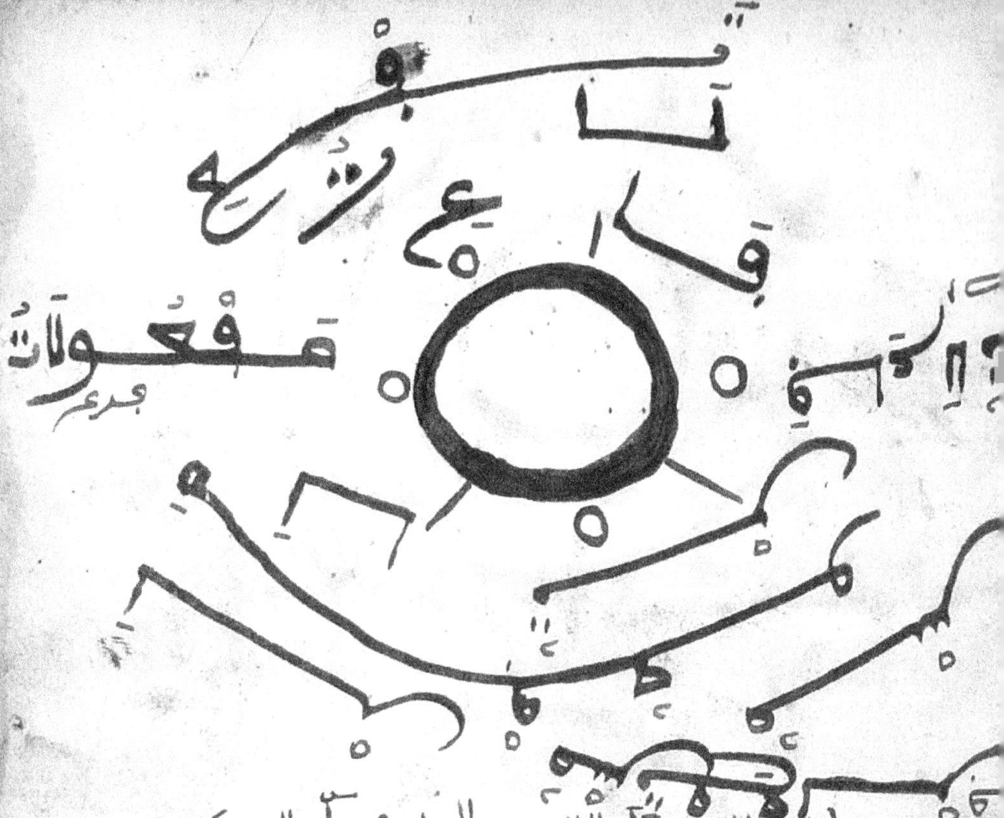

قال الخليل إذا أردت أن تنصو بالجزء في دائرة من
هذه الدوائر الأربع فابدأ بالعض أوّل من الوتد أوّل
فيخرج لك جزء ثم تشغل الأول السبب الخفيف
الوتد فيخرج لك جزء أيضا ثم تشغل أيضا الأول سبب
أخرى فكأن هكذا تفعل في الجميع إلا أنك لا تجوز
هكذا

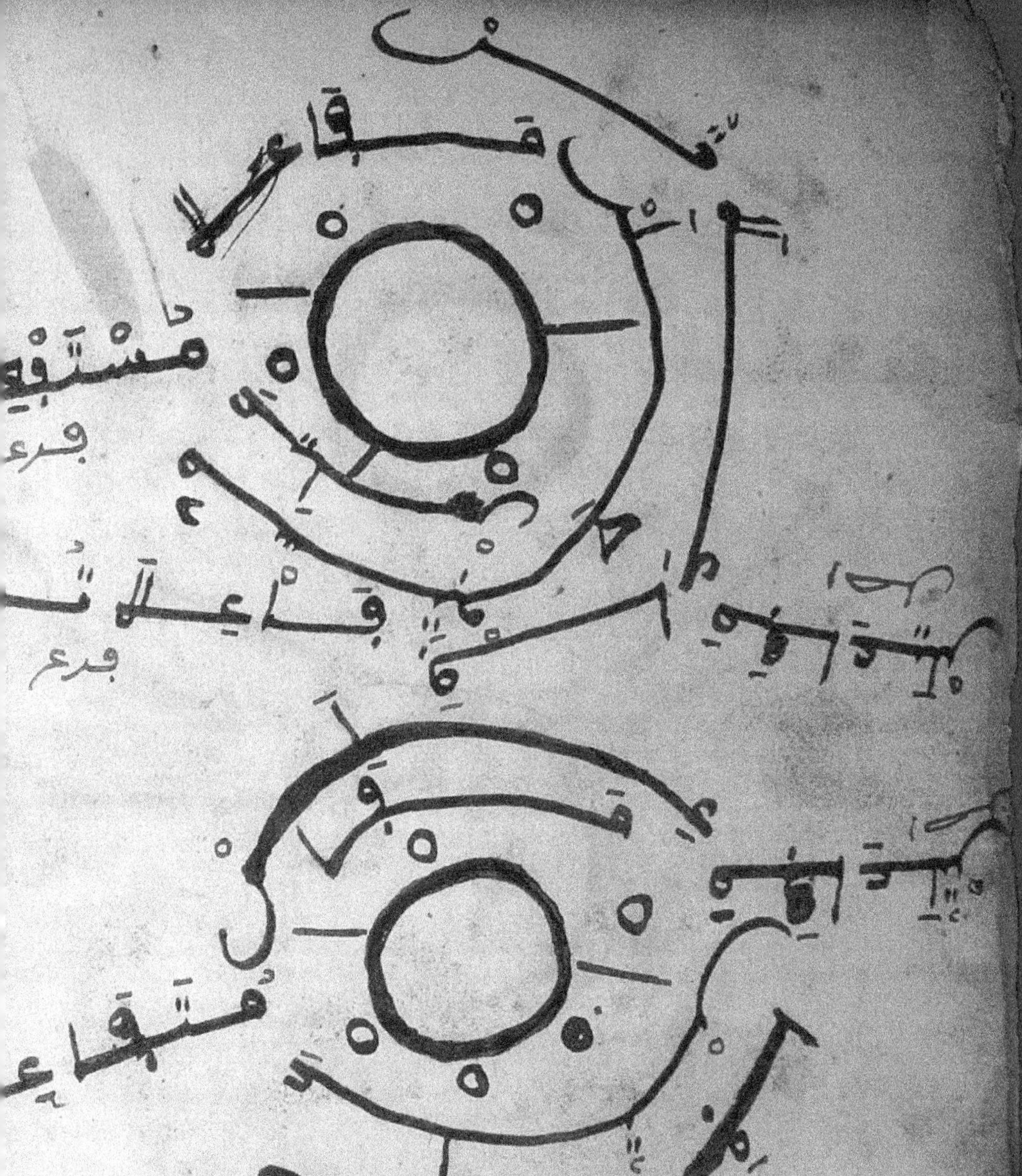
فرع
فرع

Preceding pages:
Treatise on Arabic metrics (16th century)
An illustration of Al Khalil's circles, an 8th century scholar who codified a system of versification in Arabic.

Excerpt from a manuscript on the occult sciences (kutub al-asrar) containing three magic squares (wifq) and including Indian numbers.

[illegible] الر [illegible]

[illegible] السماء [illegible] وعلى [illegible]

[illegible] الاصحاب [illegible] القلب [illegible]

[illegible]

[illegible]

[illegible] وتعرف [illegible]

[illegible]

[illegible] حوائجه فيسهل [illegible]

بسم الله [illegible] الرحمن [illegible] الله [illegible]

[illegible] الالباب [illegible] وعلمه [illegible]

[illegible]

[illegible] الا [illegible] شاء الله وهي [illegible]

[illegible] الا [illegible] فتعلو الله [illegible]

[illegible] علما و [illegible]

[illegible] كهم الله وهو [illegible] العليم [illegible]

انه [illegible] الله [illegible] كما [illegible]

وهذا [illegible]

[illegible]

١٨٤	٩	١١٢	١٨٤
١٩١	١٨٨	١٨٣	٦
١٨٩	٩٢	١٨٧	١٨٧
١٨٨	[illegible]	١٨٥	[illegible]

The Manufacturing of Knowledge

The way that knowledge was "manufactured" at Timbuktu was unlike all other education systems that preceded it. Contrary to rumor, it was not a university properly speaking but a cluster of about a hundred schools scattered throughout the city.

The basic precepts of the Quran were taught to everyone from the youngest age. Among other things, this strengthened the students' skills of memorization. During his visit to Timbuktu in 1506, Leo Africanus was literally enthralled by the ability of the students he met to recite entire passages of the Quran by heart. He was also astonished to observe algebra lessons being taught to young children. In fact, there was no discipline that did not require skills of memorization. While Europeans relied upon mnemonic devices to assimilate the Analytics of Aristotle, students at Timbuktu memorized texts in poetic verse form. The most recent treatises in logic, Al Maghili's *Rajaz* or Al Murawanaq Abd Rahman Al Akhdari's the *Sullam* (1414-1416) were composed in verse form, so they would be easier to learn.

Afterwards, the students were admitted to a *madrasa*. The most gifted would pay to continue their studies in a *durus*, a sort of school established in the homes of the most renowned men of letters. It was there that law was taught and the learning they had acquired began to be organized to their benefit. Public acknowledgement of their learning was granted in the form of a certificate called *ijaza*, which included an exhaustive list of the works they had read and learned.

From that point forward, they competed with their peers in the educational setting of the *silsila*. Here, students sought to attach themselves to the most renowned scholars by offering to assist them; for their part, the scholars sought to identify the most gifted students in order to further their own reputations.

This game was well suited for those with social ambitions, and it compelled future diplomats to gain considerable knowledge from seven or eight different masters.

The student then chose a single teacher who remained his mentor for life.

This academic practice, which was replicated in the Orient and North Africa, illustrates the referential nature of the "university" of Timbuktu; however, it also explains why so many scholars wanted to teach there. In reality, only a few families boasted a large number of scholars, among them the *Akit* and the *Anda Ag Muhammad*, both families of Berber origin. These families would "provide" the most suitable mentor from its various brothers, cousins, and nephews. Al Sa'di, author of the *Tarikh al-sudan*, refers to a scholar from Cairo who came to Timbuktu where he hoped be a professor; however, after gaging his own level of education, he set off for Fez to further his studies before returning to teach in Timbuktu.[1] According to George Hardy, rector of Alger and author of *Vue générale de l'histoire d'Afrique* (Armand Colin, 1942), it was precisely "this excess of zeal among Muslims for perfecting the art of teaching, especially in Sudanic African, that escaped the attention of the first Christians in the region, i.e. the Europeans."

On the other hand, this same zeal in the heart of the Sudan was the reason its light shone so brightly throughout Africa; it was also the reason why Timbuktu grew into such an important center of commerce.

Today, the various manuscripts held at the Ahmad Baba Library enable us to gage how Timbuktu's educational system enabled scholars to rise above the precarious conditions of everyday existence and to gain the respect of others.

At Timbuktu, the transmission of knowledge was first and foremost a matter of talent and morality. Whatever wealth one gained resulted from this. The following anecdote tells the story of a certain Abdullah Ibn Umar, a renowned man of letters. One day, the slaves of this scholar took an unusually long time milking the cows and so sold the cows' milk after dark, which is rigorously forbidden in Islamic law. Since he didn't know how much money his slaves had made that night, but wanting to leave nothing to doubt, Abdullah gave the entire sum to the poor in order to be absolved from all possible sin. This act earned him honor and respect: by custom, the *ulemas* set the standard, and they made their good deeds known through eyewitness accounts. This brought them good luck for the future.

A scholar could therefore even grow wealthy from their learning (in fact, he was encouraged to do so in order to avoid corruption), but he was also required to remain within the limits of public morality if he wanted "God's blessing." What he gained is popularly referred to as *baraka*...

For all practical purposes, there was nothing that could not be bought and sold in Timbuktu. Students could take courses in law (*figh*), grammar, rhetoric, logic, astronomy, history, and geography. According to Professor Jean-Louis Triaud,[2] the need for books was so great that "an industry developed very early for

1.Joseph Cuoq, *Histoire de l'islamisation de l'Afrique de l'Ouest*, Geuthner, 1984.

2. Centre d'études du monde africain, Université de Provence.

copying works that were sold in the North." Above all, there was a demand for "abstracts (*muskhtasar*) and exegetical commentaries (*sharh, hashiyya*), in effect mnemonic devices employed by professional scholars. " Certain classics, Triaud notes, were known only by way of "tree diagrams with commentaries that were written by local scholars; their aim was to elucidate the literal meaning of the words employed."

The libraries of Timbuktu and surrounding areas are filled with these sorts of "memory aids." In some cases, these abstracts could undermine the claims of students or scholars who sought to pass themselves off as men of learning.

As evident in written correspondence found in Timbuktu's libraries, this great thirst for learning confirms the osmosis that occurred between Arabo-Sudanese civilization and ancient Egyptian civilization. Between 1450 and 1591, Timbuktu was the glorious epicenter of this osmosis. It was as if the desert concealed a great secret, holding some memory of ancient Egypt's genius in perpetuity.

Much later, in the 18th century and near the beginning of the 19th century, the entire Sub-Saharan region, especially Mauritania, profited on a smaller scale from the further entrenchment of this knowledge, largely due to the successful efforts of the big nomadic tribes with men of learning, particularly the Kunta.

"Those who do not want to die young or become an orphan should write the name of God on an amulet and pin it on their chest."

بسم الله الرحمن الرحيم

باب ومن اراد لا يموت

احد ولا يكون ينتد او

يموت صبيا فتكتب اسم الله

الاعظم وعلقه له على الصبي

العمر ولا يتضرر ان شاء الله ان

الله اصطفى لكم الدين

ولا تموتن الا وانتم

مسلمون تمت

باب ومن اراد ان يجرب الرجال النساء

تكتب هذه الاسماء وجعله من لانه و

الكلب ترى عجبا

ويطبه

ج ههههه بداهه

Specific Characteristics of the Manuscripts of Timbuktu

The works of Timbuktu are distinguished by the fact that they often consist of separate folios that are not bound with any cover or leather container. Although these folios are often paginated without *raqqas*[1] on the lower page, they are preserved in the original order established by their authors; this fact speaks well of the *ulemas* and students of the Sudan who do not content themselves with perfect mastery of the Islamic sciences, but instead systematically memorize the texts that they study. Additionally, many of these manuscripts contain marginal notes that, placed end to end, are veritable chronicles of day-to-day life in Timbuktu.

These manuscripts are written in Arabic but also *ajami*: texts written with Arabic characters but pressed into the service of African languages such as Pulaar, Swahili, Wolof, and Hausa. In effect, assimilation of the Arabic language necessarily led to adequate mastery of calligraphic forms of expression to facilitate local needs.

Constant Hamès notes that, "After a long period of incubation in the 13th and 14th centuries, when scholars from many different lands dwelled in Songhay, the reign of the first sovereigns undoubtedly occurred at a time when local peoples had assimilated the language and ideas of the Arabs. Having reached this threshold, they could now turn their attention to more local forms of literary production."

After his residency of eight months in Timbuktu in 1352, Ibn Battuta confirms that the first erudite and literary body of indigenous African language writing in Arabic appeared from the earliest days of the Songhay Empire. As true with Latin in Western Christendom, the Arabic alphabet enabled African Muslims to import and export written texts and many new ideas. In Souleymane Bachir Diagne's view, however, the Arabic language also played a key role in shaping the imagination of those who lived in Timbuktu.

The sheer volume of manuscripts discovered in Timbuktu, but also in Chinguetti, Jenne, Oualata, and Niger, suggests that an entirely new mindset had come into being. Scholars sought from the Quran some explanation for the transformation in the local cosmology that had taken place. Why did African peoples now find themselves in this position? Understandably, theology and mysticism assumed an important place in providing an explanation for this shift, as amply documented by these manuscripts. Even so, philosophy, or the asking of ques-

1. *Raqqas*: a word that normally appears at the beginning of the following page.

tions outside an Islamic framework, had always existed in Timbuktu. Proof for this can be found in a manuscript discovered by John Hunwick, entitled *Futuhat al Rabbaniyya*. It was written in 1828 by the nephew of the famous scholar Muhammad Bello. The same year that the Frenchman René Caillié found a city that he described as "nearly abandoned," an *ulema* from Timbuktu was busy writing a work of philosophy that offered a critical analysis of the various conceptions of life among materialists, naturalists, and physicians, including further reflections upon the transitory nature of the world, the existence or non-existence of spirit, and the nature of the celestial spheres" ...

The scientific body of work that accumulated in Timbuktu between the 13th and 14th centuries is essentially nomadic in character. If knowledge was produced in Timbuktu, it was also widely imported and exported in diverse places beyond the region. Thanks to the copyists, manuscripts from Timbuktu circulated in Cairo and Grenada, Gao and Arawan, as well as Mecca and Bornou. The works of the Greek philosophers of Antiquity were carried on the backs of camels traversing the desert in caravans. Evidence of the existence of local copies and scholarly analyses of the writings of the ancient Greeks were discovered at the Sankore Mosque of Timbuktu, dating from the late 19th century.

It is clear, in any event, that a vast number of these manuscripts reflect Timbuktu's high level of intellectual productivity.

In the 14th century, "extraordinary phenomena" were often investigated, such as a scholarly study of geographical configurations and natural climatic phenomena. This particular work was the product of several scholars who lived in the region, a patrimonial line that included the celebrated Sharif Sidi Yaya, a scholar whose name is associated with one of Timbuktu's most important oral traditions.

There is even a treatise on astronomy that was composed in verse in the Saharan manner (a manuscript held at the Ahmad Baba Center). Three copies in good condition from the 9th, 16th, and 17th centuries, treatises on geomancy, philology, and chemistry, also demonstrate the vast disciplinary fields and variety of research that was performed (a manuscript held at the Ahmed Baba center provides details on the chemical preparation of a compound from lead and red arsenic).

A colophon, or the last page of a manuscript, with information about the owner of the manuscript.

بحمد الله وحسن عونه اللهم

اغفر لي والوالدي ورحمهما

كما ربيار صغيرا اللهم ا

غفر الجميع المسلمين

والمسلمات والمو

مين والمومنات

امين

امين

امين

صاحب

هذه

كتاب

الصدر

تب ابراهيم

تب احمد

لمة تر و

ومعالمه

يغفر لي

ابا حمد تب بلد

باكرو فيلا جنبة

Alexander At Timbuktu

by Georges Bohas

I present here three excerpts of the history of Alexander the Great from a manuscript found at Timbuktu. These excerpts will be included in a longer work I am currently editing and translating along with Ahyaf Sinno (Saint Joseph University in Beyrouth), and Abderrahim Saguer (the University of Agadir).

An excerpt from a manuscript entitled *The Novel of Alexander* is held at the Mamma-Haidara Library. As true of the popular novel in general, its author of this novel is unknown. Based upon its composition, it probably dates from the 18th century.

The Yemenite Origins of Alexander

It is often said that he was a Tubbaa,[1] one of kings of Yemen. It is also said that he was a virtuous saint of God and that God loved him. He was a young and intelligent man, who trusted the divine order. He was a man of letters, well versed in the science of the law. He was favored by fate, a man of discerning spirit and opinions, with a penetrating gaze. He affirmed the unity of God; he kept God's holy days[2] and assiduously applied God's Law.

One day he wrote a letter to Tubbaa of Yemen. His letter began with these words:

"In the name of God who created the wind and the sky!"

But the king was angered by these words and replied to him:

"If you do not place my name before the name of the creator of the winds and the sky, I will most certainly put you to death."

He swore to it with all pomp and ceremony.

The Two-Horned replied, "By God, I will never place the name of a creature who is unable do either good or evil on his own before the name of the creator who is responsible for bringing evil and good alike into the world,[4] who has power over all that He wills.[5] God, who is without parallel.[6]"

This only increased the ire and wrath of the king who now threw him into prison. When night came, God caused lightening to strike this king, engulfing him in flames and reducing him to cinders. His spirit vanished into the fire. The Two-Horned thanked God for what He had done. Afterwards, the Tubbaa's subjects agreed to elect him as successor to the king. He therefore became their king and ruled them in the best possible manner, giving them the best possible orders, and conducting himself in the best possible way, all on their behalf. He ruled so well that he was named Tubbaa himself, as if he was of the same origin as the Tubbaa who had thrown him into prison.

Why Is He Called The Two-Horned?

God sent him to His creatures endowed with the rank of Messenger. He sent him to his people so that he could call God's creatures to His religion and reveal to them God's signs, so that he might clarify God's proofs on their behalf and teach them that God has power over all things, that His science extends to all things, that He is the Ancient, the Eternal who is without coexistent partner, that He is The Ancient, The Perpetual, who created all things out of nothing. But his people treated him like a liar. They stormed him, seized him, and violently beat him. They hit him so hard on his right horn that they broke it, causing his death. God brought him back to life, awakening him from his sleep in order to send him back to his people. As happened the first time, he bestowed upon them orders and prohibitions that were so upsetting that they beat him once again. This time, they broke his left horn, and he

1. Pre-Islamic Yemenite Dynasty. This exotic origin will not surprise those who are familiar with legends about Alexander. In *The Apocalypse of the Pseudo-Method*, the mother of Alexander is none other than Kouchat, the daughter of Pil, King of the Kouchites. See Bohas, 2009, *Alexandre syriaque*, Lyon, ILOAM, page 99.

2. In other words, Divine Providence

3. Surah The Table, 76.

4. Surah The Deliberation, 29.

5. Surah The Deliberation, 11.

6. Sourate La Répudiation, 12.

died from the injury. Then God brought him back to life, and at the site of his two horns there were now two thick tufts of hair, hard as iron, covering his entire head. No sword could cut these tufts of hair, save by the power of God. That is why he is called the Two-Horned.

Alexander and the Indifferent Old Man

Kaab said:

"Then, he walked to Jabalqa and, when he arrived, he ordered the horns to be sounded and the trumpets to be blown." Not a single one of the inhabitants failed to come outside to witness the arrival of the Two-Horned and his soldiers.

Then, the Two-Horned noticed an old man busy at work. When the Two-Horned passed by him, the old man did not pay any attention to him.[7] Alexander was so surprised at the old man's behavior that he ordered him to be brought before him. This man was devout. When he was in presence of Alexander, he said to him,

"What do you want with me?"

The Two-Horned replied,

"Oh, Old Man, the army that accompanies me is the army of God. Why did you not look up at me and my royal entourage as we passed?"

He replied,

"All your gold and royal entourage made no impression on me."

The Two-Horned then asked him,

"Why not?"

The Old Man replied:

"Because I am the son of a king, and it happened that my father and a poor man died on the very same day. We buried them together. After a number of days, the tomb collapsed and we found both of them together. Their bodies and shrouds had greatly altered. Their flesh had become detached and was now mixed up in one heap. You could no longer distinguish one man from the other. This is why your royal entourage does not impress me. If God wants you to enjoy a happy fate, then you will be a happy man. Otherwise, you will know regret. Reflect carefully upon these two options. Choose the fate that will bring you riches, or choose the best of all possible fates.

Then the Two-Horned said to him,

"Old Man, tell me how much you earn each day with the labor of your hands?"

"A dirham," he responded.

"And how do you spend it?"

"I divide it into three parts. With the first third, I pay my debt to my elderly parents because they spent their money on me when I was little. The second third I send to someone who has racked up a debt to me, my own son. If God wills that I should enjoy a long life and if I fall into need, he will repay the money that I loaned him. I myself live on the last third, as well as all those to whom I am duty-bound."

Amazed by these words, the Two-Horned replied,

"I proclaim here today that you are a wise man, and that it is incumbent on me to name you governor of this town, for it is obvious that you will never abandon God's decrees."

After investing him with power, he ordered the townspeople to obey the old man's in each and every instance.

7. This is no doubt the Arabic version of the history of the encounter between Alexander and Diogenes.

Oblivion: Myths and Prejudices

In the 14th and 15th century, the Songhay Empire was transformed into an enchanted cultural space that was shielded from outside greed for the simple reason that no one really believed in its wealth.

Throughout the entire 15th century, Timbuktu also contributed to the rise of its own myth, but it could do so only insofar as doubts remained about its economic and cultural reality.

The importance of Timbuktu's commerce in salt and gold was well known. (In Mali today nearly sixty tons of salt per year continue to be extracted from the earth.) The fact that a great number of students and scholars lived there was also well known outside the region. (At the time, there were a hundred and eighty Quranic schools that produced manuscripts.) But, in Morocco, as was true in the Orient and Occident, the accounts of travelers (and few of these were actual scholars) were insufficient to foster belief in the high degree of civilization that the Songhay had attained. In fact, the culture that the Songhay created may have overshadowed its Arabian and European counterparts.

In the *Description of Africa*, written in 1526 and cited previously, Timbuktu is described as follows: "In Tombutto there are many judges, doctors, and priests, who are discretely appointed by the king, for he holds scholars in great esteem. Many of the manuscripts that are sold here end up in Barbary. More profit is gained from their sale than all the other merchandise combined." This observation must have attracted some attention outside the region. But the Occident did not have a great deal of interest in Africa at this time. At this point in history, Christian Europe was decimated by a plague from China that killed more than twenty million people. In these circumstances, few thought of much more than their daily survival. Thanks to improved farming techniques and increased agricultural yield, the "urban" revolution had also taken off. Europe's values gradually began to change. Before this era, "an agrarian economic shaped the daily rhythm of one's life," Daniel Cohen has observed. "There was no haste, no worry about precision, no anxiety about productivity." [1] From this point forward, the life of Europeans "would be regulated according to strict timetables," Le Goff notes.[2] In the meantime, the population of hunter-gatherers in Islamic Africa continued to

1. *La Prospérité du vice*, Albin Michel, 2010.

2. *Un autre Moyen Age*, Gallimard, 1999.

uphold their magisterial animism and to give precedence to the "humanist" fate of those they met up with in their own backyards. As observant Muslims, they cultivated their own notions of solidarity, hospitality, and wisdom.

From this point forward, the two civilizations increasingly ignored one other. In the 16th century, Erasmus in his *Plea For Peace* asserted that only those who lived in Christian lands could truly be happy – proof positive of Europe's superiority. The real difference between the two civilizations was Europe's invention of the printing press. After moveable type was invented, it seemed inconceivable to most that writing even existed outside the port cities of Amsterdam or Bordeaux.

We must return to the 12th century to grasp how the most unfavorable prejudices came to be associated with Africans, referred to at this time as "Ethiopians" (from *Aethiops*, meaning "burnt face" in Greek).

For the Christians – apart from a small minority of Catholics who, under the religious guidance of Father John, affirmed the inherent wisdom of black civilization – black people were commonly said to descend from the line of Ham, the cursed son of Noah. This color, associated with darkness, evoked for them the frightful powers of demons from hell, even Satan himself. This era marked the end of ecclesiastical efforts in the 12th century to promote rationality in education, championed in France by the School of Chartres and the Scholastics. In the 13th century, theologians like Albert Le Grand or Roger Bacon now rose to the forefront of church debates on science and religion. Dogmatic and literal interpretations of the Bible undermined the necessary conditions for the circulation of new ideas.

As Jacques Le Goff has observed, it is remarkable that Occidental travelers, merchants, and missionaries of the 14th century could have been so audacious and curious, yet when they fixed their gaze upon Africa they "were never really saw it." Le Goff adds, these travelers were "burdened with the weight of too many previous representations." No doubt Europe's dream of possessing Africa's gold and salt, augmented by its desire to penetrate Islamic lands and convert African peoples to the "civilizing" virtues of Christianity, was the true impetus behind these travelers' audacity.

In 1631, the celebrated *Mercator and Hondius* atlas definitively fixed[3] the name of Timbuktu on the map. From then on English explorers, and later French colo-

3. In 1373, Charles V issued a relatively obscure printing; in 1413, another printing was made by the Majorcan Jew Mecia de Viladestes.

nizers, nurtured only one ambition: To conquer this myth but without bothering to understand the people who lived in these lands.

The true history of the region would remain unexplored until the 20th century when Octave Houdas, at that time Professor at the School of Oriental Languages at Paris, translated the celebrated *Tarikh al-sudan* into French in 1913.

Although late in appearing, light was now cast upon the actual history of African civilization, a history that was written by an African for Africans; however, the appearance of this translation barely received any notice in France. Some historians and Africanists (Maurice Delafosse, for example) were interested in this book's appearance, but far more were too busy playing their part in a civil and military colonial adventure at its apex. There was little effort to even modestly rethink an established Occidental ideology that was firmly anchored in Cartesian certainties. The elites and the adventurers preferred myths to realities. The rest clung to their prejudices.

However, the eminent scholar Houdas could certainly not be faulted for his lack of audacity. In the introduction to his translation of *Tarikh al-sudan*, he boldly sought to prove the scientific importance of this late appearing historical discovery (a history of the Sudan that included the rise and fall of the Songhay Empire). "[This document] shows that these populations, commonly described as lacking all initiative in matters of progress, indeed developed a civilization of their own," he wrote. "This civilization was not the external graft of some other race. Furthermore, the disappearance of this prosperous State is largely due to conquerors of the white race. Today, this indigenous history must take its place within the greater history of all humanity, a grouping of nations that has hitherto been completely excluded from all consideration..."

In 1955, the American academic John Hunwick exhumed two texts from the second half of the 16th century on the military Islamization of Bornou: the *Kitab Ghazawat Burnu* and *Kanem*. Additionally, he discovered a section of the personal library of the famous Ahmad Baba of Timbuktu (1556-1627), who left behind a considerable body of work (thirty-two volumes). These works included biographies of scholars and enormously important scientific works on questions of law. Today, they enable us to better understand the high levels of learning that were attained by the *ulemas* during this era. For instance, a manuscript of Saharan character, written by Ahmad Baba, speaks of the virtues of knowledge (number 776, dated 1702). This work, like many others, has only been accessible since 1973, the date of the Ahmad Baba Center's opening in Timbuktu. But this means that for a great many generations, Sub-Saharan African peoples, who have for so long been regarded as ignorant and illiterate, were not only cut off from their own history, they were also oblivious to the contributions that their ancestors had made to humanity at large.

Today, it is quite difficult for younger generations to fully grasp the power of the book, of texts, and knowledge in general at Timbuktu from the 14th to the 17th centuries. One reason for this is the deeply engrained nature of the culture of orality in the African imagination. What is at stake is not so much proving that Africa's long-standing writing traditions offer irrefutable proof that it once enjoyed a "golden age," but asking why only random traces of this heritage are known today. The dearth of scientific exploration is, in this case, rivaled by poverty in translation.

The Timbuktu researcher Saad Traore, a graduate of the Practical School of Advanced Studies and a specialist in codicology, emphatically states that, "for many generations, a phobia of pillage has existed. During the Moroccan invasion in 1593, the Moroccans burned down the library of Ahmad Baba; then Colonel Archinard, the Governor and official representative of French colonizers, did the same to the Al-Hag library of Umar Tall at Segu. From then on, local inhabitants felt compelled to hide their manuscripts, to protect them in crates; later, they tended to forget their existence."[4]

During the first archeological mission to the Sudan in 1912, the Frenchman Georges de Gironcout had great difficulty convincing local inhabitants to open their trunks. He saw only one hundred and ninety manuscripts, too few to deduce the vast scope of this heritage. During his residency in the Sahel, those he spoke with convinced him that "the Sudanese did not write their own history," but orally transmitted it.

"What I inform you of now," Gironcout documents from the mouth of a local resident, "was transmitted to me from the ancients, who learned it from their ancestors, and so forth and so on. Our customs are not like your customs, for our way is to learn through memorization." As Saadou Traore notes, Gironcout deduced from this exchange little more than the myth of African orality, not the very real fear that he too might pillage manuscripts that belonged to the local population.

The myth of Africa's exclusive orality has also been reinforced by the sage

4. Thesis submitted in April 2011 under the direction of Francois Deroche.

Amadou Hampate Ba who, speaking more as a prestigious Malian diplomat than as a writer himself, famously stated in the mid-20th century that "when an old man dies in Africa, it is like a library burning down." The downside of this memorable saying, which loudly reverberated in the halls of UNESCO, was that it tended to exclude Africa from inclusion in the written societies of the world.

The traumatization that occurred in the aftermath of the fall of the Songhay Empire, following the Moroccan invasion, also compounded this situation.

The Moroccan occupation, which was mandated by the Sultan Moulay Al Mansour in 1590 in order to acquire the salt mines of Taodenni, culminated in the blood baths of 1603. This historical event left a bitter taste in the mouths of the local populations. It also left Europeans with the false impression that this region was a sort of *tabula rasa*. Meanwhile, the transplanted populations of local Tuareg and Roumas (Moroccans who stayed in the Sudan after the invasion), after years of killing one another, decided at last to abandon the city to Barbarian forces. All that was remained in Timbuktu was devastation.

By the end of the 17th century, it was no longer a matter of asking about Timbuktu's wealth, its gold, salt, books, and scholars. The question now was rather, "How could an entire civilization have collapsed in less than a century, leaving so few traces behind?" Moreover, the manifest evidence of this civilization was from now on denied, concealed, looted, or forgotten.

As for the Arabic language, it is understandable why this language was so seldom taught or inculcated after the Moroccan invasion. In fact, the specter of its existence in the Republic of Mali today continues to stir up a collective malaise in the Sub-Saharan imagination.

One proof of this is that, for almost twenty years, the director of the famous Ahmad Baba Center of Timbuktu does not know Arabic, although the funds that he oversees are intended for the scientific preservation and investigation of manuscripts written in the language of Averroes.

Until very recently, there was little reason to believe that this impressive Arabic language archive, whose existence was known by all but rejected, might be able to awaken the outside world – as if by magic – to the reality of Africa's ancient civilization.

In the courtyard of the house of Abdel Kader Haidara of Timbuktu.

Underestimated Inventions and Writing Practices in African History

By Doulaye Konate
Professor, University of Bamako
President of the Association of African Historians (AHA)

As V. Y. Mudimbe once put it, "Africa was the invention of Europe." He alluded in this case to the epistemological methods that the Occident employed to "construct" an image of Africa, skewed as this image was by colonization and the trans-Atlantic slave trade. Africa has always been viewed as an "a-historic" continent, as Hegel famously remarked, because it did not possess writing. Instead, Africa was considered to be "an exclusive reservoir of oral traditions." The enduring image of Africa as the "world of the spoken word" is so difficult to shake that many African writers, even those of the highest rank, appropriated this *idée recue* and even celebrated it.

Africa's historical reality is far more complex. In the first place, it is important to note that *all* civilizations, including those said to possess "writing," also have oral origins. For a longtime, Europe has functioned on two separate registers, two different systems of measurement. As Amadou Mathar Mbow reminds us in his preface to the eight-volume collection *l'Histoire générale de l'Africa*, Europe relied upon its own major oral works, like the *Illiad* and *Odyssey*, to establish its historicity. The writings of Homer effectively contributed to the establishmnent of a chronological framework for understanding the history of ancient Greece (the Trojan war described by Homer has become an essential signpost of Occidental history). The importance of Homer, in this reading, lies in the fact that Homer is said to have merely transcribed Greek traditions that had previously been orally transmitted, albeit with a certain literary talent. African oral traditions, on the other hand, have been judged as far less reliable sources of history; they are viewed as the product of local "fetishers." If African societies indeed possess rich oral traditions, they have also constantly preoccupied themselves with the preservation of cultural memory on behalf of posterity through the use of writing. Apart from the emblematic example of Egypt, which can quite nicely be situated in an African context rather than construed as some weightless abyss, as many like to think, there are countless instances of writing's invention and deployment throughout Africa's long history. Besides the obvious example of the Egyptian hieroglyphs, one might cite numerous instances of authentic Africa writing, including Ge'ez script, one of the oldest writing systems in the world (the language of the ancient Ethiopians continues to be used today as a liturgical language in the Ethiopian Church), the Meroitic (an alphabetic writing system invented by the kings of Meroe, an outgrowth of Egyto-Nubian civilization flourishing in the geographical region of modern-day Sudan between 590-340 C.E.). Closer to our own era, shortly before the era of colonial penetration, the Sultan NJoya in the country of Bamum, in Cameroon, invented Bamum writing with the goal of fostering literacy and scholarship in his kingdom on a massive scale.

African peoples have also taken advantage of foreign languages (and their alphabets) that were introduced on the continent to transmit local memories and heritages. As a case in point, Islamicized Africans have often written their own historical chronicles, i.e. accounts that follow a chronological ordering of events of their own era, or older eras orally reported to them. The chronicles of Kilwa in East Africa, written in Swahili, are among the best known of these. One might also cite the Kano chronicles from northern Nigeria and, of course, the chronicles that were written in Timbuktu in Mali (in the 16th and 17th centuries).

The greatest of these are the *Tarikhs* of Timbuktu, the *Tarikh al-sudan* ("Chronicle of the Sudan, the land of the Blacks") and the *Tarikh al-fattash* ("Chronicle of the Seeker"), written by Black Sudanese "Arabists." Both are authentic African sources on the history of the Western Sudan at the time of the great West African empires. There is a long-standing and well-established tradition of Arabic language manuscript production in West Africa. In regions situated more to the south, the "*Tariqa*" tradition arose in connection with Islam's expansion. Today, many families in the great Islamic bulwark towns of West Africa have in their possession family chronicles that remain guarded secrets and that document each individual family's historical linage. In addition to these writings of a wholly private character, there also exist across West Africa important literary works in the vernacular language that have been transcribed with Arabic characters (most notably, poems exalting the saints and other charismatic religious leaders). This is the case with poems written in Pular in the Futa Jalon (Guinea), dedicated to the illustrious persons of Islam, the "Kassidans" among certain Hamalists (the adepts of Shaykh Hamadullah) or the *qasidas* ("odes") of the Muridiyya of Senegal.

Apart from religious settings, a form of writing was once again "invented" in West Africa in the 1940s (by a Guinean named Solomana Kante), called "NKo", today the basis for a cultural movement of the same name that is very active in the sub-region and that calls for mass alphabetization based upon this writing system.

In 1999 in Mali, a week was consecrated to local alphabets and systems of signification, which demonstrated the importance of indigenous scriptural traditions and sought to foster awareness among those populations inheriting them. A Bamana proverb asserts that, "writing is the storehouse of memory." However, there have been significant obstacles undermining the wisdom that is encoded in collective sayings like this about the virtues of writing in African society. These include limited access to the foreign manufacturing of books, the lack of availability of publications in the national languages of Africa, but also the inertia that comes from force of habit.

What seems more fundamental to me is the way that writing continues to be perceived in the African imagination. This perception has long been influenced by colonial administrative practices that rejected the oral tradition in favor of writing, even in cases where the spoken word was more reliable than the written word. The colonial educational system accordingly created a chasm between all those who knew how to read and those who didn't. Writing thereafter became a tool of social discrimination that facilitated colonial domination. Since all writing is linked to some system of thought, gaining access to foreign languages seemed in the eyes of many Africans the surest possible means to enable their child to find a place in an entirely different universe.

In the context of the diaspora, Africans were literally beaten for their mastery of writing. In this case, writing was a means for transmitting knowledge that demonstrated the "vulnerability" of Africans, the problematic nature of their very "being in the world." The question to ask then is whether or not writing mastered in foreign languages and the discursive forms that issue from these languages can truly allow African peoples to articulate their "vulnerability." As Bougumil Koss rightly notes, "Africans who are able to pick up the pen in order to create their own representations of themselves are first burdened with the need to affirm what they are not, to restore their right to speak as subjects endowed with agency." It is precisely "on a terrain that they do not perceive as their own" that African peoples must rediscover their own lost agency.

This is one reason why the manuscripts of Timbuktu are so important today. They are "sites of cultural memory" that provide evidence of the decree of excellence achieved by the ancients. They also demonstrate why it is important that African peoples today must affiliate themselves with African forms of writing.

أمير الله [illegible] بسنة يشنو [illegible] عامنه أبكر [illegible] إمر
وقانف إذ متذ مسيد خد في لا كل [illegible]
الفتنة الله [illegible] بر رجل الأمير رحم [illegible]
[illegible] فوت [illegible] لا با [illegible] الهو اجز [illegible]
[illegible] سعد رجا [illegible] ليل الحمر لا شك قليل ولا شيء
بر كو ق في التابيه ابن الحج بلا ست يرج [illegible]
بر عبي العلموم قبسر جلا الحمر فكيد [illegible]
بر [illegible] رعية العلم [illegible] بسر [illegible] الخيل [illegible]
الصلاة قر [illegible]
الدنيا جمة ابة وكلبه كلب لا شك ما كر الله
قمم [illegible] بلا قر بكر [illegible] الله [illegible] كل
ما [illegible]
نو رذل الحي [illegible] ومرشي اذ حمر يا [illegible]
التراع [illegible] الهو ق [illegible]
الدنيا [illegible]
و [illegible] ترج [illegible] ترتبرا وجو [illegible]
[illegible] جه لنا سيف فوجشفه [illegible] محمد [illegible]
[illegible] لا خفر اما [illegible] وهو [illegible]
[illegible] عنعو [illegible] جربه يا [illegible]
جسي نا اغم [illegible] ما [illegible] بج [illegible]
[illegible] بلا وزي [illegible] ترتبه [illegible] الشه [illegible]
قادة [illegible] فيتر [illegible] زبور [illegible]
اكنا عمي [illegible] تورت [illegible] علي [illegible]
[illegible] شك [illegible] الله [illegible]
الله [illegible] فلا [illegible] الابتر [illegible]
[illegible] الفو [illegible] نحو [illegible]
[illegible] عند [illegible] ليك [illegible]
[illegible] يه [illegible] بلدا [illegible] الو [illegible]
جميز [illegible] اتناي [illegible] فتنا منسه [illegible]
[illegible] الصلاة الله [illegible] جنه [illegible]

On Mali's Written Heritage

By Doctor Mahmoud Abdou Zouber,
Historian

If it is true that Mali is a land where orality predominates, it remains no less true that the writing appeared in Mali at an early date and has played a key role in the affirmation of the cultural identity of many local populations.

The Tuareg (a Berber group living in the north of the country) seem to have been among the first peoples to master writing in the region. The Tifinagh alphabet, which was in use long ago, probably dates to the end of the Neolithic period.

However, there is no doubt that Arabic writing is the most striking instance of writing in West Africa. Islamization of the region effectively began in the 8th century of the Christian era. Its arrival led to the wide diffusion of this form of writing, thanks to the construction of mosques in the principle towns, as well as Quranic schools and "universities." These institutions fostered literary production and therefore the building of numerous libraries, both public and private, containing thousands of manuscripts. These documents on every topic imaginable are largely written in Arabic.

Unhappily, not all of these documents were passed down to us, mainly due to fires and pillaging. Yet, in spite of the ravages of time, many regions of Mali today continue to hold important collections of manuscripts. The Malian government and the international community have worked together to save these manuscripts from destruction, including the efforts of the Ahmad Baba Center of Timbuktu and the owners of many private libraries.

At present, nearly sixty thousand manuscripts have been assembled although some five hundred thousand manuscripts in total are said to exist in the region.

Some of these documents are original works that are particularly valuable for the information that they include on the political and social history of the Sudano-Sahelian region.

This written heritage enables us to observe how that history has been constituted over the ages.

When Islamic culture was first introduced in the Sahelian Sudan, probably in the 8th century, it expanded rapidly in the big villages like Walata, Timbuktu, Gao, and Jenne. This occurred during the rise of the Empire of Mali in the 14th century but reached its apex in the 15th and 16th centuries with rise of the Songhay Dynasty of the Askiyas. It was during this epoch that written documents authored by Sudanese people of the black and Berber race first appeared. The most celebrated of these documents is no doubt the biographic dictionary of Ahmad Baba (*Nayal al-ibtihaj bi tatriz al-Dibaj*).

This work, which was composed in 1596, contains information that is completely original on the cultural history of Occidental Sudan and that casts a light upon the role of Arabic literature in this part of Africa.

In effect, it enables us to follow the intellectual development of the Sahelian Sudan over two centuries (the 15th and the 16th). This dictionary describes the schools and "universities" frequented by so many students. It also provides information in Arabic about the books that Sudanese professors adopted for instruction, including those from universities in the Maghreb and the Orient. There are also descriptions of the region's relatively considerable libraries, of princes and caravans of pilgrims that left Timbuktu each year for Mecca.

The other three major texts that enrich our written heritage were written in the 17th and 18th centuries. These are the *Tarikh al-sudan* by Abderrahmane Al Sa'di, the *Tarikh al-fattash* by Qadi Mahmud Kati and Ibn Al Mukhtar, and the *Tadhkirat al-Nisyan*. Along with the *Nayal al-ibtihaj* by Ahmad Baba, these unparalleled works stand today as the most important African accounts bearing witness to the general history of the Occidental Sudan up to the 18th century.

The importance of the *Tarikhs* lies above all in the fact that they provide information that is all the more precious because it comes from well-informed witnesses to the major political events of their time. Al Sa'di and Mahmud Kati alike served as public officials over a long period of time and both played important roles as trusted advisors of the Songhay political and military leaders.

The *Tadhkirat al-Nisyan*, which is an anonymous work written in the 17th century, is equally important not only for its wide scope, but above all due to the unique nature of information it provides on the Moroccan presence in the Sudan. Its focus is the era of the Moroccan pashas at Timbuktu from 1590 until 1750.

During the second half of the 18th century, there is a significant resumption of intellectual activities nearly everywhere in the Sahelian Sudan, which led to a time of abundant literary production. The Kunta and Kel Al Suq (two nomadic tribes of marabouts) played a very active part in this cultural renaissance. One might also cite the names of Shaykh Sidi Al Mokhtar Al Kabir, Shaykh Sidi Ali Al Najib, Muhammad Al Suqi Al Daghughi, the *Qadi* Talibna Al Wafi, Sidi Muhammad and Ahmad Al Bakkay. These intellectual figures dominated the 18th and 19th centuries.

A single Kunta family is credited with producing more than five hundred literary works, some extending over several volumes. These works include all types of genres. These writings are epistolary, religious, historical, poetic, and legal in nature

For their part, the educated Fulani, including those from the Futa as well as the Macina Fulani, have bequeathed a considerable amount of literary work to posterity, both in Arabic and Fulfulde. These include works such as the *Rima* of Al Hajj Umar Tall, the *Qasida* in Pulaar by Muhammad Aliou Thiam, the circulated letter of Alfa Nouh Tahirou on the subject of the succession of the twelfth caliph in the Sudan, the *Tabki al-Bakkay* (a satiric work) by Alfa Yerkoy Talfi. All these works, which were authored by the Fulani, constitute enormously significant contributions to the written heritage of Mali.

Finally, we cannot omit the important poetic writing in Tamasheq, Songhay, and Fulfulde that may be found in the outlying regions of Mopti, Timbuktu, Gao, and Kidal.

It is also important to note the historical value of the epitaphs of Gao, Adrar of Iforas, and in the valley of Telemsi. These inscriptions not only tell us something about the Islamization of these regions, they also reveal much about the historical relations between the kingdoms of Gao and Andalusia in the 11th and 12th centuries of the Christian era.

In conclusion, we affirm here that a deeply established tradition of Arabic language teaching, as well as instruction in the Islamic sciences, flourished for many centuries in the main towns of the Sahelian Sudan. This development enabled a great many men of letters and scholars to write works on a wide variety of subjects. Many of these documents are now lost to humanity due to the vicissitudes of history and the elements. Others risk following suit if urgent action is not taken, so that they may be assembled, preserved, catalogued, and then carefully studied.

In order for this to happen, the manuscripts must be divided into stable and transportable units so that each work may be properly enumerated.

Additionally, there is an urgent need for the creation of a research team consisting of West African, Maghrebian, and other regional specialists for the scientific exploration of these documents that contain so many new and hitherto unpublished facts of the highest significance. Doing so would offer irrefutable proof that Sudanese peoples had indeed attained great cultural maturity, and that they were fully capable of writing their own history and reflecting upon matters of law, logic, medicine, theology, astronomy, and grammar.

The shelves of the Mamma-Haidara Library.

Bibliography

Ahmad Baba, *Kifayat al-muhtaj il ma'rifat man laysa fil-Dibaj*, Manuscript Number 1430, CEDRAB.

August Cherbonneau, "Essai sur lat literature arabe au Soudan, d'après *Takmilat al-Dibaj*," in l'*Annuaire archéologique*, of Constance, II (1854-1855), pp. 31-42.

Mahmoud Zouber, *Ahmad Baba de Tombouctou (1556-1627). Sa vie et son oeuvre*, Maissonneuve and Larose, Paris, 1977.

ID, "Les écrits en langue arabe," in Revue *Notre libraire*, 1985, numéro special consacré à la literature malienne.

A FAMILY LIBRARY AT TIMBUKTU

مكتبة مماحيدرة للمخطوطات والوثائق
BIBLIOTHEQUE
DE MANUSCRITS
MAMMA HAIDARA
TOMBOUCTOU
BP. 71 TEL: 292 16 76

Abdel Kader Haidara and manuscripts from his library.

A manuscript on the virtues of collective worship.

فصل ووقف بعد وامام الجمع ... الاكثر بالعمر ... والصفين
الصف الاول ... والبحر ... على القوابل والله تعالى اعلم ... [illegible]

فصل على قول هذا ... جواز اكل النعم ... [illegible]
[illegible] ... يكون ... على قول ... [illegible]
يكون ما القصر ... [illegible]

فصل وعن النبي صلى الله عليه وسلم انه قال اتاني جبريل عليه السلام فقال
يا محمد ركعة واحدة يركعها المومن مع الامام خير من الدنيا وما فيها وعلى ...
وتكبيرة يكبرها المومن مع الامام خير له من مائة رقبة يعتقها ... فقال ...
يا جبريل ما للمصلي في صلاة الجماعة من الاجر فقال يا محمد اذا كان رجلان كتب الله
... ثلاث مائة صلاة واذا كانوا اربعة كتب الله ...
... صلاة ... التكبيرة الاولى خير ... من الف ...
... اذا كانت الجماعة عشرة كتب الله ...
... الف صلاة واربع مائة صلاة يا محمد فقال ... على العشرة ...
... الشجر اقلاما ... ما قدروا ان يكتبوا ثواب ركعة
واحدة من صلاة ... الجماعة وقال النبي صلى الله عليه وسلم حرمت الجنة على ...
مفارق الجماعة وحرمت الجنة على امراة ... زوجها ... وحرمت الجنة
على من كان في قلبه مثقال حبة من الكبر وحرم الله الجنة على من سب ... وقال
صلى الله عليه وسلم اخبرني جبريل عليه السلام ان المومنين ... [illegible]
الملائكة ... للمومنين ... من ... الاخبار ... [illegible]

المرضى ولا كلها فان السحر يذهب عنه بقدرة الله والباب المرضى
صفته ان ياخذ شيئا من الثياب الكميت ويجعل في اناء نظيف وياخذ عودا
او غيره يحرك به الثياب ويقرا عليه قل هو الله والمعوذتين ولقد جاءكم
الى اخر السورة وننزل من القرءان ما هو شفاء لو انزلنا هذا القرءان
على جبل لرايته خاشعا الى اخر السورة يستعملها ان يفعل ذلك سبعة
ايام يكتب له مع هذه الشكاة حرزا يعلق عليه وهو بسم الله الرحمن
الرحيم الحمد لله رب العلمين الى اخر السورة والهكم اله واحد الله لا اله
الا هو الحي القيوم لا تاخذه سنة الى والله سميع عليم امن الرسول
الى اخر السورة شهد الله الى وهو العزيز الحكيم لقد جاءكم رسول الى اخر
السورة قل ادعوا الله او ادعوا الرحمن الى اخر السورة وننزل من
القرءان ما هو شفاء ورحمة للمومنين قل الله اذن لكم ام على الله
تفترون واذا ذكرت ربك الى نفورا واذا قرات القرءان الى مستورا
لو انزلنا الى اخر السورة اذا زلزلت الارض الى اخرها قل هو الله
والمعوذتين يعلمون الناس السحر الى باذن الله اللهم لا تجاوز
ولا تسلط كل جبار جبار فلان بن فلان لا اسمه واسم ابيه يحفظك كل
سحر وشر كل انس وجان واسئلك اللهم باسمك الاعظم وكلماتك
التامات التي لا يجاوزهن بر ولا فاجر ان يمنع بهذا الحرز المكتوب لمن
يكون فيه من شر الانس والجن وشر ما علم منه وما لم يعلمه الا انت
والساكنة وجميع ما فيه برحمتك يا ارحم الراحمين وصلى الله على سيدنا
محمد وءاله وصحبه وسلم تسليما كثيرا الى يوم الدين انتهى والنبات
المتقدم ذكره ينفع لجميع الامراض صفة استعماله ان يجلس في الشمس
قليلا ويدهن به الموضع الذي فيه الوجع فيبرا باذن الله انتهى فصل

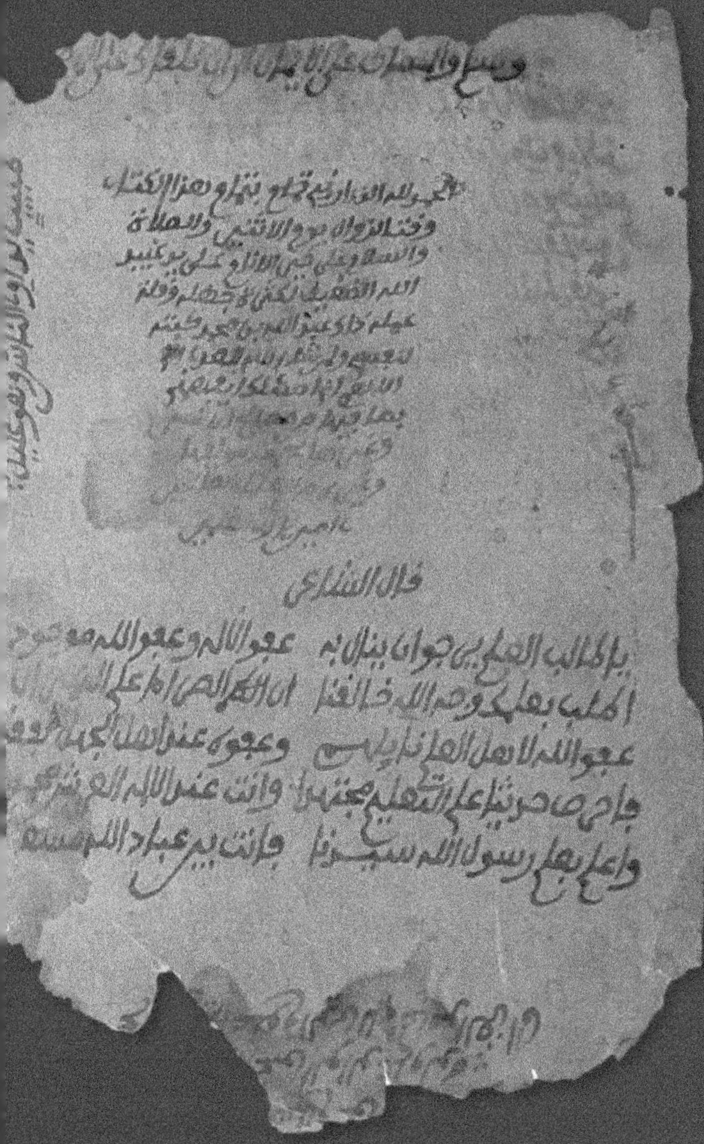

Kitab Masalih al-Insan al-Mutaliqat bi al-Adyan wa al-Abdan (Human Concerns About Religion and the Body).

Author: 'Abdullah Ibn Muhammad Ibn Usman Ibn Fodio (1245H/1892G)

Theme: The rights and duties of man towards himself and towards his fellow man during the various stages of his life.

Copyist: Abdullah Ibn Muhammad

Number of folio: 26

Number of lines: 19

Dimensions of the written text: 8.5 x 13.7 cm.

Dimensions of the cover: 11.9 x 17.5 cm.

وان لاربع نهارية ـــــ او

ليلية غير المقيمة رووا

قد طهرت صلتهما او لا فل

سقطت الاولى على ما قد قبل

وضابط المذكور ان تقطعن

تقدير الاولى ركعة كذا ازكن

وكل منهما متى حاضت لذا

سقط ما قد ادركته فخذا

فيسقط الفرضان في حيضتها

لخمسة من يوم او ليلتها

ولا فلا راع تفصيلا عنا

بغاب الا ادراك فاجر له هنا

Number 3905: Jazwat al-Fayd min Muhimat al-Hayd ("The Heat of the Menstrual Cycle")

Author: Muhammad Ibn Al Mukhtar Ibn Ahmad Ibn Abi Bakr Al Kunti Al Wafi (1242H/1829G)

Theme: This manuscript addresses the topic of the female menstrual cycle, both its positive and negative aspects.

Type of writing: Sahrawi.

Color of Ink: Black and red.

Number of folio: 8

Number of lines: 12

Dimensions of the written text: 7.5 x 12.4 cm.

Dimensions of the cover: 9.9 x 14.2 cm.

A manuscript with magical formulas for defeating one's enemies, for arousing a woman's love, and for stirring up ill-feelings.

[illegible] لك	فتحنا	مبينا	[illegible]
ق[illegible]	يا [illegible]	يا [illegible] حبيب	نشرحيق
هو الواحد القهار	ملك فتاح	صاحب	ن تام
[illegible]	رحيم رشيد	ذهبي جواد	

الاصباح و[illegible]
عمل بمثل ال[illegible]
وقضى ربك الا[illegible]
اللخر والسموات الل[illegible]

اللوح الثامن لدفع الاعادي والغلبة على الخصماء جيدا جيدا وهو هذا

فسيكفيكهم	الله وهو	السميع	العليم
عال مجيد	جواد منع	يا صبور [illegible]	صبر [illegible]
يا وكيل	يا غ[illegible]	[illegible] حلي	يا [illegible]
يا نافع	فلا احسبيا	حي رزاق	بهي ديان

اللوح التاسع وهو حرز من العيون الضارة والله جلبيتوكي امنه مجرب لكل ضلع منه عم عم عم وهو هذا

حسبنا	الله	ونعم	الوكيل
عزيز	سابق	محيط	[illegible]
محيي	قابل واحد	مصلك	باعلاء
مانه	وهي	حبوب	ديان

اللوح العاشر لعطف القلوب والتهييج والمحبة وتليين القلب القاسي وهو مجرب في كل ضلع منه ٦٦٦عم وهو هذا

يحبونهم والذين امنه	نعصهم عليه لعب	كحب محبة الخمير	الله منى لشديد
يا منيب	يا لا اله الا الله يا الحي يا احد	يا منعم يا جواد	يا راشد يا وفي
يا نافع يا وهاب	يا سيد يا شكور	يا رقيب [illegible] مجيد	يا الله يا قاهر يا محصي
[illegible] يا عظيم يا واحد يا جواد	يا عالم يا بصير	يا باقي يا شفيق	يا هو يا معافي

اللوح الحادي عشر للبغض وايقاع الفرقة والعداوة بين اثنين مجربا في كل ضلع منه ٦٦٨٧ وهو هذا

والقينا	بينهم	العداوة	والبغضاء
الى يوم القيامة	لا اله الا الله	[illegible]	عالم قيوم
طمسنا	الرحيم	جارع [illegible]	[illegible]
احد [illegible]	عظيم [illegible] اخر	حصل نعمي	حاج اول

اللوح الثاني عشر للوسوسة وان اضر الهموم والافكار الردية وهو حرز من الجن والشيطان عجيب في كل ضلع منه ١٩١ وهو هذا

لا حول ولا قوة	الا بالله	العلي	العظيم
رجال [illegible] احيا [illegible]	مالك موجود	صاحب	صاحب الشرف [illegible]
هبيس	اول رحيم مستقيم	[illegible]	والي وفي
عزيز ماجد	يا هو [illegible]	[illegible]	[illegible]

اللوح الثالث عشر يصلح للنصرة والظفر على الاعداء في كل ضلع منه ٥٠[illegible] وهو هذا

نصر	من الله	وفتح	قريب
حي رابع	احد قد بر معين	باطن مطلع	هو [illegible]
محس	فارسطل	عبا[illegible]	قدر [illegible] جواد
[illegible] عابر	[illegible]	ناصر	دابع

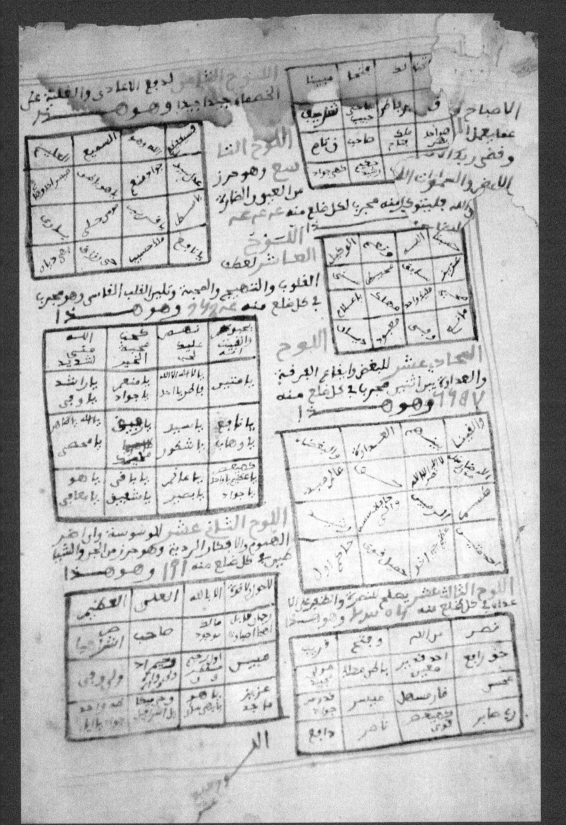

ال

A magic square for obtaining material goods. The text insists on the necessity of repeating certain formulas such as, "Lord, grant me Your forgiveness."

فعلمه	وخلق	[illegible]	اخرىاه	يسمعه	اجمه	عشعه	ازقه	فا	ياهوم	ارا	لسعه	[illegible]
وخلق	عليهم	اخرىاه	يسمعه	اجمه	عشعه	ازقه	فا	ياهوم	ارا	لسعه	[illegible]	فالن
عليهم	اخرىاه	يسمعه	اجمه	عشعه	ازقه	فا	ياهوم	ارا	لسعه	[illegible]	فالن	[illegible]
اخرىاه	يسمعه	اجمه	عشعه	ازقه	فا	ياهوم	ارا	لسعه	[illegible]	فالن	[illegible]	مو
يسمعه	اجمه	عشعه	ازقه	فا	ياهوم	ارا	لسعه	[illegible]	فالن	[illegible]	مو	[illegible]
اجمه	عشعه	ازقه	فا	ياهوم	ارا	لسعه	[illegible]	[illegible]	[illegible]	مو	عشعه	اللهم
عشعه	ازقه	فا	ياهوم	ارا	لسعه	[illegible]	قالن	[illegible]	مو	عشعه	اللهم	رب
ازقه	فا	ياهوم	ارا	لسعه	[illegible]	قالن	[illegible]	مو	عشعه	اللهم	[illegible]	اللهم
فا	ياهوم	ارا	لسعه	[illegible]	قالن	[illegible]	مو	عشعه	اللهم	رب	اللهم	يرزق
[illegible]	ارا	[illegible]	قالن	[illegible]	مو	[illegible]	اللهم	رب	اللهم	[illegible]	[illegible]	مو
ارا	لسعه	[illegible]	قالن	عشعه	مو	الله	رب	اللهم	يرزق	مو	[illegible]	يشاء
[illegible]	[illegible]	[illegible]	[illegible]	[illegible]	اللهم	اللهم	رب	يرزق	مو	يشاء	[illegible]	بغير
[illegible]	قالن	[illegible]	[illegible]	عشعه	اللهم	رب	اللهم	يرزق	مو	يشاء	بغير	حساب

اللهم لا اله الا هو الحي القيوم لا تاخذه سنة ولا نوم له ما في السموات وما في الارض
من ذا الذي يشفع عنده الا باذنه يعلم قال ابو الحسن الشاذلي رحمه الله [illegible] وسالته
بسم الله وبالله ومن الله والى الله وعلى الله فليتوكل المومنون حسبي الله اكتفيت بالله
ورضيت بالله توكلت على الله لا حول ولا قوة الا بالله اشهد ان لا اله الا الله وحده لا شريك
له واشهد ان محمدا عبده ورسوله رب اغفر لي وللمومنين والمومنات الحمد لله
رب العالمين الى اخرها واقول امين واقل الحمد لله وسلام على عباده الذين اصطفى
مرة ثلاثا او خمسا او سبعا او عشرا او بالعشرة بعدد هذا سر لا يعطا [illegible]
ثم قل رب اني ظلمت نفسي ظلما كثيرا ولا يغفر الذنوب الا انت فاغفر لي وارحمني
وتب علي لا اله الا انت سبحانك اني كنت من الظالمين او خيرته [illegible]
الى سميع [illegible] حكيم وضياء كريم [illegible] قل [illegible]

لاعلي

بسم الله الرحمن الرحيم صلى الله على سيدنا محمد
وآله وصحبه وسلم تسليما

الحمد لله الذي أنعم علينا بنعمة الإيمان والإسلام
وهدانا بسيدنا ومولانا محمد عليه من الله
أفضل الصلاة وأزكى السلام

أما بعد فكتاب أصول العدل لولاة الأمور وأهل
الفضل فأقول وبالله التوفيق إن أصول العدل عشرة
كما قال الغزالي في بعض تواليفه وأورد كلامه على
وجه التلخيص والاختصار مخافة التطويل الموجب الملل
الأصل الأول أن تعرف أيها السلطان أولا قدر الولاية
وتعلم خطرها فإن الولاية نعمة من قام بحقها نال من
السعادة ما لا نهاية ولا سعادة بعدها ومن قصر
عن النهوض بحقها حصل في شقاوة لا نهاية لها
ولا شقاوة بعدها إلا الكفر بالله تعالى ومما يدل على
عظم قدر الولاية إن كان السلطان عادلا قوله عليه
الصلاة والسلام عدل السلطان يوما واحدا أفضل من
عبادة سبعين سنة وقوله عليه الصلاة والسلام والذي نفس
محمد بيده إنه ليرفع عمل السلطان العادل إلى السماء مثل
عمل جملة الرعية وكل صلاة يصليها تعدل سبعين
ألف صلاة وقوله عليه الصلاة والسلام المقسطون
لهم في الدنيا على منابر اللؤلؤ يوم القيامة ومن ...

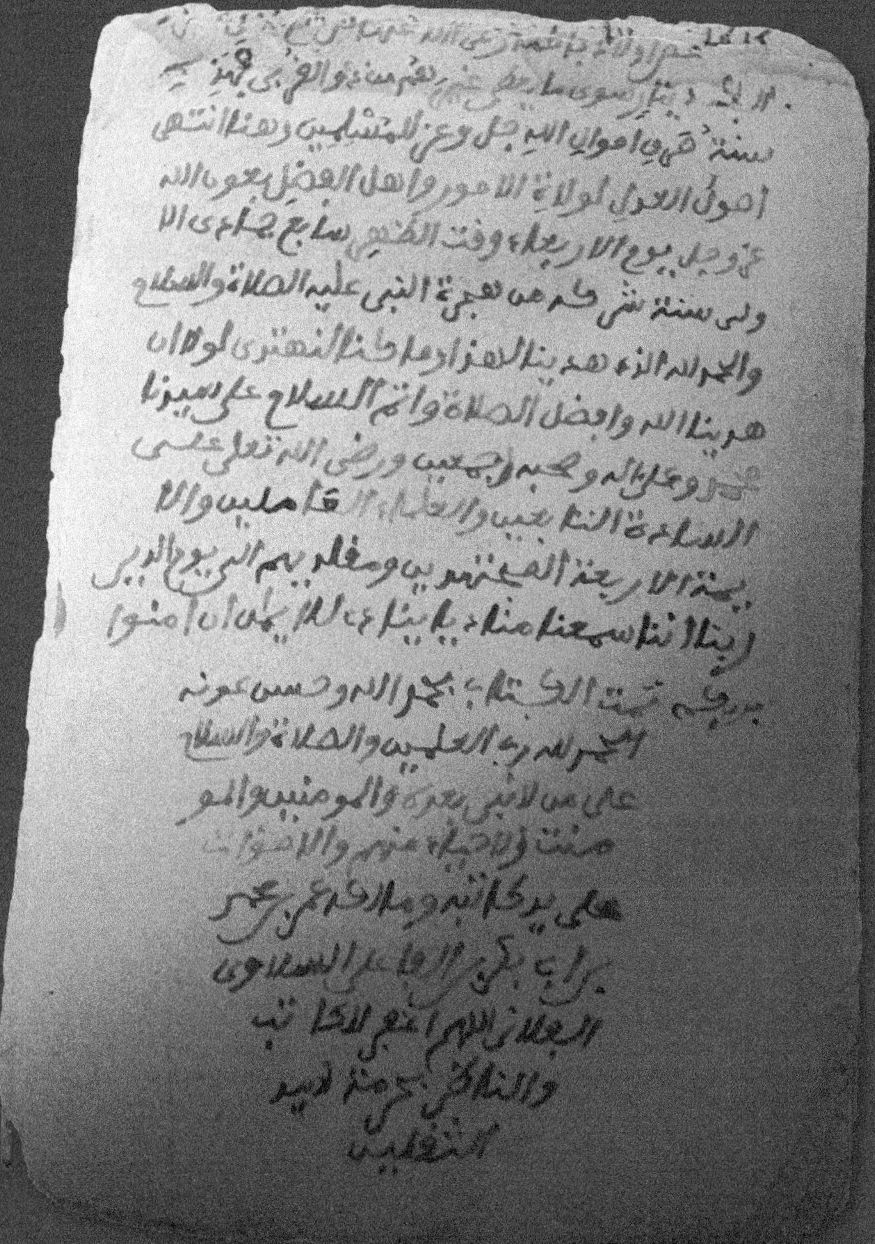

[illegible]

سنة فهي أقوال الله جل وعز للمسلمين وهنا انتهى

أصول العدل لولاة الأمور وأهل الفضل بعون الله

عز وجل يوم الأربعاء وقت الظهر سابع جمادى الا

ولى سنة [illegible] من هجرة النبي عليه الصلاة والسلام

والحمد لله الذي هدينا لهذا وما كنا لنهتدي لولا أن

هدينا الله وأفضل الصلاة وأتم السلام على سيدنا

محمد وعلى آله وصحبه أجمعين ورضي الله تعالى عن

[illegible]

ربنا إننا سمعنا مناديا ينادي للإيمان أن آمنوا

بربكم [illegible] الكتاب بحمد الله وحسن عونه

الحمد لله رب العالمين والصلاة والسلام

على من لا نبي بعده والمؤمنين والمؤ

منات الأحياء منهم والأموات

[illegible]

Number 3443: Usul al-ʿadl li wulati al-Umur wa ahl al-Fadl ("Principles of Fairness On Behalf of the Responsible and Virtuous").

Author: ʿUthman Ibn Muhamad Ibn ʿUthman Ibn Fudio (1233H/1817G).

Theme: Good Governance

Copyist: ʿUmar Ibn Muhammad Ibn Abu Bakr Al Fa'ili Al Salawi Al Fullani

Type of writing: Sudani

Color of ink: Black and red

Number of folios: 6

Number of lines 22

Dimensions of the written text: 9.3 x 15.6 cm.

Dimensions of the cover: 11.5 x 17.3 cm.

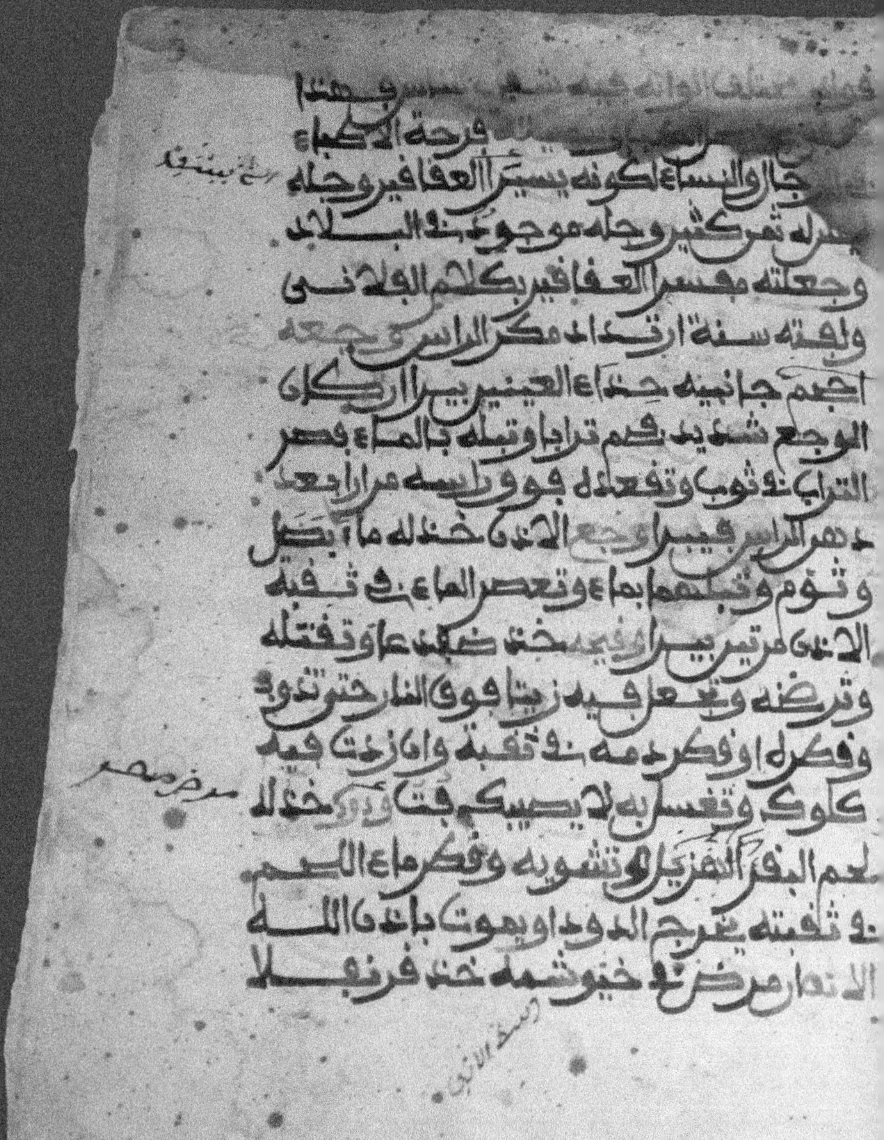

[Description of images on pages 162-163, appearing on the bottom of both pages]

Farhat al-Atiba fi al-Rjal wa al-Nisa ou Farhat al-Atiba wa Rahat al-Fuqara ("The Delight of the Doctors At the Good Health of the Poor")

Author: Ahmad Ibn Baram Ibn Nuh Baba Ibn

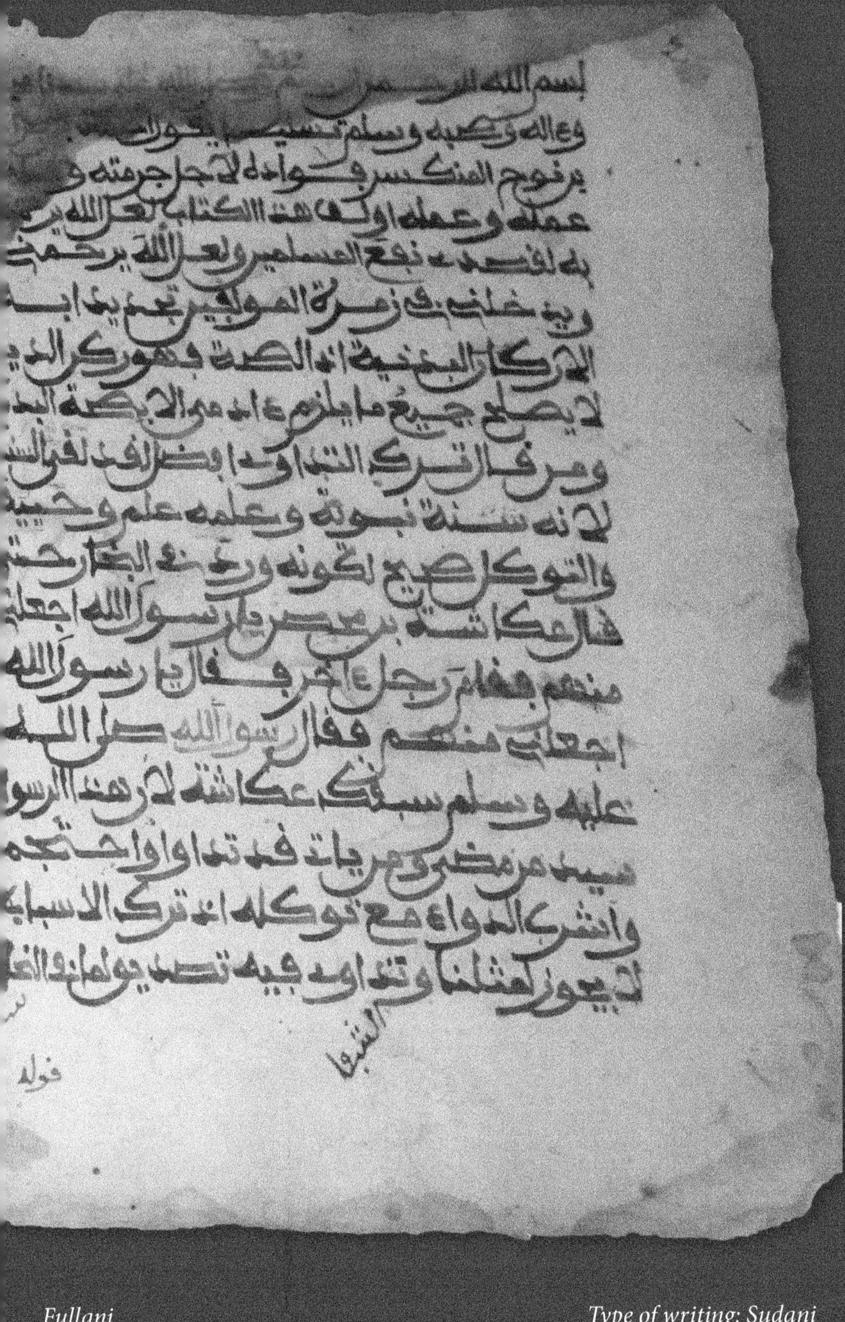

Fullani

Theme: Medicine. This manuscript describes certain illnesses and their remedies. It discusses methods of treating the poor in ways that they can afford.

Date of composition: 1247H/1831G.

Type of writing: Sudani

Color of ink: Black and red.

Number of folios: 9

Number of lines: 18

Dimensions of the written text: 7 x 11 cm.

Dimensions of the cover: 15.8 x 22 cm.

Inkwell and reeds. Instruments of the copyist.

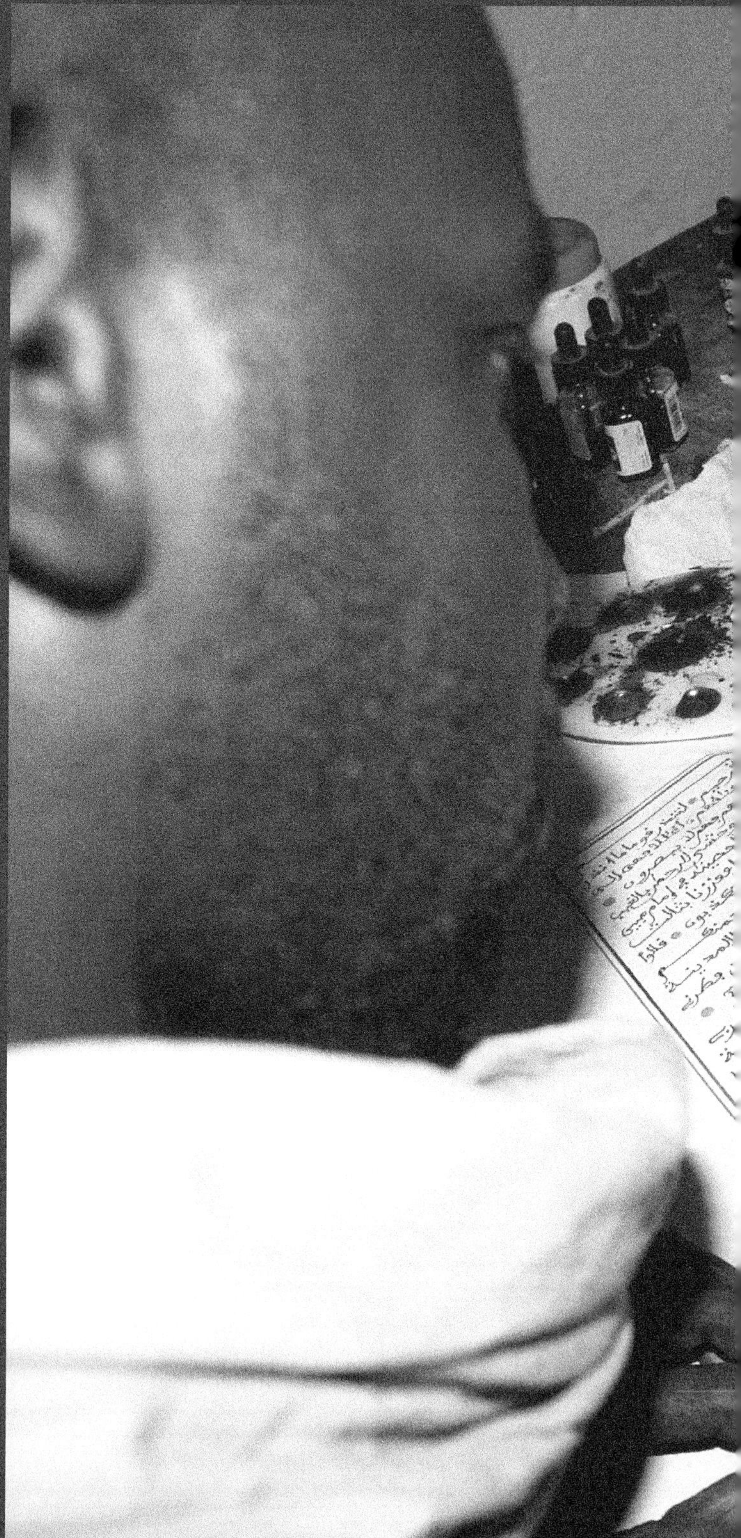

At copyist at his trade in Timbuktu.

Conclusion

The myth of Timbuktu is inextricable from the myth of its writing. One is associated African mystery, the other with African civilization. In both cases, our Christian and Arabo-Muslim cultures have encouraged the outside world to discount the historical significance of the manuscripts of the City of 333 saints.

But the specificity of a written source containing so many rich details, buried in a city that is widely perceived as "exotic," cannot leave History unaffected. For this reason, we must briefly revisit the question of Timbuktu's "cultural diversity," a phrase that is so often championed by the world's democracies that see in it a counterbalance to the destructive impacts of globalization.

But how can we appreciate this cultural diversity if we are not aware of it, if we do not gage its deeper significance? As true both now and in the past, there have always been fluxes in migration patterns causing duress to those impacted. Time and again, the peoples of Africa have felt compelled to uproot their lives. Like their ancestors before them, many today have migrated from the region leaving few visible traces behind.

Some examples

Antar (Antara Ibn Shaddah Al Absi) was an Afro-Arab warrior-poet, who died in 615 before the coming of Islam. This man is the hero of a celebrated epic tale that is entitled *The Novel of Antar* (10 volumes, 1865-1877; *Antar, the Novel of a Beduin*, 4 volumes, 1819-1820). Some of the verses in this great work make reference to his African origins. Prejudice about skin color is evident at various places in the text.

The black poet Abu Dulama Ibn Al Jaun, who died in 777, also composed verses for the Abbasid court of Baghdad.

Ziryab (Abdul Hassan Ali Ibn Nafi), an Afro-Persian sometimes referred to as "the Black Rossignol," went to Spain in 1822, where he made a significant contribution to the evolution of its poetry, especially to the poetry, music, and songs of Andalusia.

Both of these poets were born slaves. Yet who remembers their writings today?

What is the point of revisiting History, it might well be asked, when nation states that once made a lively contribution to the world's production of ideas now find themselves incapable of upholding Africa's shared destiny, a half-century after independence?

Before the 15th century, the territorial hegemony of the Ghana Empire, and then the Empires of Mali and Songhay, laid the foundations for West Africa's many diverse civilizations. It is remarkable that this occurred at all, given the existence of so many micro-ethnic groups in the region, the coming of Islam to a profoundly animistic world, and the region's extraordinarily difficult geo-climatic conditions. It is a good thing then that Africa really does share a "common destiny," one that is arguably more salient than that of Europe, China, or the Americas. No doubt, this is why Léopold Sédar Senghor so often spoke of the "United States of Africa." The fact that these writings exist at all in Sub-Saharan Africa, particularly in Timbuktu, is therefore far from insignificant. It is this slender thread that must be gently pulled, and then untangled at last, in order to understand the rupture that occurred between a past that now seems so opaque and a present that is unable to speak for itself. By translating the bulk of these documents, and then assimilating them within a greater historical framework, those who perform this work may enable us to gain insight into hegemonic myths that prevail in the West about Africa's orality and tribalism. As Constant Hamès puts it, "The task for us now is to better understand Africa's general situation through the exploration of that vast Arab speaking region, which has always enjoyed high levels of literacy after having undergone Arabization. This region includes Mauritania and the Western Sahara. Both remain outside the field of Orientalist research due to their geographical remoteness from the political centers of so-called classical Islam. This region was effectively excluded from consideration, thanks to ... the desert." Moreover, "it is something of a paradox that we must seek to better understand the history of ancient Sahelian-Sudanese Africa through the writings of the Arab authors of North Africa and the Middle East, which are then translated, published, and disseminated in European languages. For in these works, Africa is typically relegated to the margins of the Maghreb and Egypt."

The world we live in today is slowly evolving. Due to the interrelated nature of intellectual pursuits now underway, as well as the instantaneous exchange of scientific data that now takes place, old prejudices have begun to give way to less arbitrary and more humanistic currents of thought.

*

"Writing is uncanny. Its appearance could not help but cause profound upheavals in the basic conditions of human existence. The transformations it caused were essentially intellectual. The possession of writing prodigiously multiplies men's ability to preserve knowledge." Claude Lévi-Strauss, *Tristes tropiques*, 1955.

More than a half-century after the publication of *Tristes Tropiques*, it is worth once again asking the question that Lévi-Strauss famously raised about humanity's "possession of writing." Since then, others researchers have contested the well-known hypothesis that written culture contributes to humanity's cognitive development. As a case in point, David R. Olson argues in his work *L'Univers de l'écrit* (Ed Retz-1998) that "oral and written societies merely differed in their manner of their thought." The eminent Canadian professor states, "It could be that the role of writing in the development of more reflective and individualistic cultures has been considerably overstated." For this reason, Jean-Francois Dortier notes in *Sciences Humaines* (September 1998) that, "we have finally reached a point where we tend to think of illiteracy as a pathology, a form of sickness."

David Olson who was a disciple of Jack Goody (who also argued that writing profoundly altered the basic conditions of knowledge's production), likewise observes that contemporary anthology has amply demonstrated that "oral cultures are much richer than it has been assumed for a longtime." In large part, this view is due to writers like Amadou Hampate Ba, who vigorously defended orality. Such views open up a new line of inquiry, for they demonstrate our need to begin reinvestigating and rewriting a broad overview of our extant oral knowledge. Such knowledge is readily available but neglected. Even so, we must to do what we can to create a *definitive* compendium of the civilization of the written word. This being the case, what remains to be said about this ancient cradle of humanity? This African universe that is able to boast of dual written and spoken heritages?

Eric Havelock, a British specialist in the literature of antiquity, has argued that, "writing enabled the conversion of an oral form of discourse, bound to the world of poetry, myth, and dialogue, into new forms of expression. Logical analysis, argumentation, and research demanding proof gradually left behind the older poetic world of storytelling." If this is so, we will need to relearn how to read history if we hope to gain access to this ancient world.

We will need to rid ourselves of the popular belief that ideas are expressed in writing with the use of symbols, which are copies of the spoken word. Writing can also express ideas through the use of ideograms and pictograms, both which serve as a kind of a roadmap for scientific information in the form of graphs and abstract signs. Since writing cannot transmit every possible intonation of the human voice, as well as moments of silence and other unspoken forms of "information," humans needed to invent exclamation points and other diacritical signs indicating the suspension of speech. Despite their differences, writing and orality are finally united in their goal of transmitting meaning.

One of Olson's most important teachers, the psychologist Jerome Bruner, asserted that there are two basic literary genres: each one characterizes two distinct modes of thought, the narrative mode and the paradigmatic mode. The first belongs to the world of the tale: it relies upon facts, personages, and the unfolding of events in time, whereas the "paradigmatic" genre relies upon proofs and causal relations, articulated in coherent and logical prose. Although the two modes have their oral and written forms, "the second is particularly important for the tradition based on scholarly research from written sources." Many examples might be cited in support of this hypothesis. In the sacred and solemn space of the church, for instance, the tone of the priest's voice when delivering his sermon is as crucial as the strength of his argument. On the other hand, those who write lectures on morality are required to assemble a structured argument, to invent phrases that can most aptly convey their intentions. Moreover, when the traveler-scholar described for an anonymous public his knowledge of plants, animals, and unknown regions of the earth, he was forced to invent new mental tools to effectively describe what he saw, to make his case and clarify his thoughts. According to Olson, his efforts to better clarify his thoughts historically constituted, "an important cognitive leap." Jean-Francois Dortier, who was cited previously, confirms this view: "When the goal of writing became the transcription of the spoken word (hardly a matter of historical necessity), early scribes were required to create the appropriate linguistic technology from nothing. New techniques enabled expression through punctuation marks (i.e. the exclamation point or question mark, enabling more precise forms of expression) relative to lexical "illocutionary" forms ("I affirm that," "One assumes here," etc.), and forms of expression of a more general nature: the hazarding of suppositions, deductive argumentation, and hypothetical assertions. These tools fostered a growing awareness of the subjective nature of certain utterances and the universality of others. All these devices helped to clarify various forms of thought, for Olson, "an essential element in the conceptual revolution ushered in by writing."

In Africa as in other parts of the world, schools today compete with the Internet. On the web, the image takes the place of writing and digitalization takes the place of paper. It does so precisely at a moment when many of our cultural values have been appropriated by elites and obscurantism. Today, younger generations in Timbuktu and elsewhere know that they have the means at their disposal to reclaim their history and to write it anew. They only need to learn how.

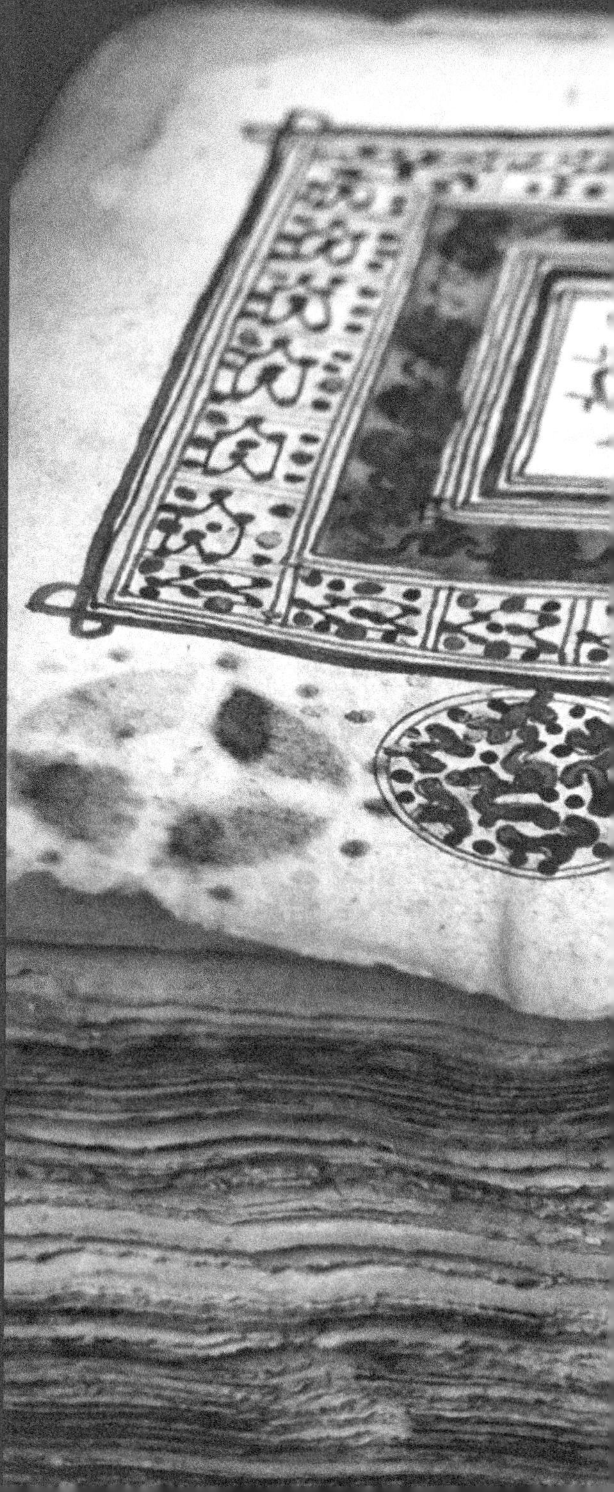

Verse 7 of the Fatiha (the first surah of the Quran).

Afterword

Souleymane Bachir Diagne

Philosophy, Professor at the University of Columbia

In his celebrated poem "Prayer of Peace," Léopold Sédar Senghor has written these verses:

And the Christians, having renounced Your light and meekness of heart
Have warmed their campfires with my parchments, tortured my talibs,
deported
my doctors and masters of science.

"Parchments"? Does he mean by this writing? Does this poet from Senegal really mean Africa, a land inextricably linked to the spoken word? Is it possible that his words "talibs" (or "students"), "doctors," and "masters of science" mean what they mean everywhere else: people who study and teach with the use of *writing*?

This is indeed the case, and it is a good thing that the poet-president says so.

The fact that Europeans were not the first to introduce writing into Sub-Saharan Africa is well known, although absently, without grasping its full significance, or taking stock of its greater import. To do so would mean rejecting the false claim that Africa is an oral civilization in its very nature and essence. In effect, it would mean taking into account the arrival of Islam on the Black continent from the earliest years of the Hijra. As Albert Gérard has pointed out, Arabic writing came into these regions to facilitate understanding of the Quran; for more advanced students, this also meant they would be instructed in the Arabic language. Quranic studies led to the rapid spread of Islam. In some settings, this resulted in the establishment of truly superior institutions of higher learning based upon the Arabic alphabet.

Of course, writing in Arabic was first and foremost the sole privilege of the scholars, those who spent more time than everyone else studying Islam, in effect, the "masters of science." Writing uniquely served the language of the Quran, and the sciences directly issued from Revelation in this context, as did jurisprudence, theology, Aristotelian logic, and mysticism. In each case, the aesthetic form of poetry was performed because it facilitated memorization.

In every instance, writing developed over the centuries in West Africa, which was at this time called in Arabic *Bilad al-sudan* ("the land of the Blacks") or simply the Sudan, at important cultural centers where doctors and masters of science taught "talibs" who were hungry for science. Above all, the talibs craved knowledge of law and theology. They copiously wrote on parchment, copying and circulating manuscripts at a time and place where books were rare. They also produced countless commentaries on the many works that they read. Many of these manuscripts have not yet surfaced.

The most highly esteemed intellectual center was undoubtedly the legendary town of Timbuktu. From the time of the 14th century, Timbuktu was an important site of higher learning in the Islamic world, where scholars from diverse lands and of many different complexions (Arabs, Berbers, Black Africans...) could gather together in order to debate, teach, and write.

Today, it is incumbent upon us to reflect carefully upon Timbuktu and its manuscripts. In fact, it is essential that we do so in order to comprehend the intellectual history of West Africa, a history that remains to be written.

The professor and journalist Jean-Michel Djian, "inventor" of the Open University of Five Continents at Timbuktu, is also the author of two magnificent biographies, one on Léopold Sédar Senghor and the other on the Mande author Ahmadou Kourouma.

It gives us great pleasure to affirm here that, with his foray into the world of Timbuktu, he has indeed performed a true service on behalf of Africa's "talibs," its "doctors" and "masters of science," so heralded by the poet-president.

L'ÉTOILE du CIRQUE

Inventory of the "Histories of Timbuktu"

(VECMAS/ Normale Sup Lyon)

Mama-Haidara Catalogue

1. *Qissat Du l-Qarnayan*, Number 4440, 39 folios. History of Alexander, the Two-Horned.
2. *Quissat al-isra'wa-l-mi'raj*, Number 1894, 55 folios. History of the Ascension of Muhammad (Compare this text with Latin versions).
3. *Qissat al-imam 'Ali Ibn Abi Talib ma'a al-'ahbar*, Number 1075, 6 folios, History of Ali and the Jewish Doctors.
4. *Qissat ba'd al-muluk wa siyarihim*, Number 2212, 76 folios. History of Some Kings.
5. *Qissat Buluqya*, Number 1936, 11 folios. History of Bulukya (An Israelite who, After the Death of Solomon Proclaimed The Coming of the Prophet).
6. *Qissat Tamim Ibn Habib al-Dari*, Number 353, 4 folios; Number 1372, 13 folios; Number 1810; 19 folios; Number 1890, 23 folios; Number 2037, 6 folios; Number 2475, 6 folios. History of Tamim Ibn Habib Al Dari. Spirited Away By the Genies, the Hero Reveals the History and Marvels of Their World.
7. *Qissat Tawaddud al-jariya*, Number 717, 108 folios, Number 219, 25 folios. History of the Sympathetic Scholar, a Figure from *The Thousand and One Nights.*
8. *Qissat al-jumjuma*, Number 1311, 7 folios. History of the Crane (An Allusion to a Miracle of Jesus)
9. *Qissat jamal Haybar*, Number 1066, 8 folios; Number 1103, 7 folios; Number 1104, 7 folios. History Of the Camel of Haybar (Life of the Prophet).
10. *Qissat al-Hajjaj ma'a al-gulam*, Number 1507, 3 folios; Number 2484, 4 folios; Number 2524, 8 folios. History Of Al Hajjaj and the Boy (Umayyad Era).
11. *Qissat al-Hasan al-Basri wa ma kana min Haditih ma'a al-a'jami*, Number 54, 54 folios. History of Hasan Al Basri (A Mystic and Figure from *The Thousand and One Nights*).
12. *Qissat al-Hasan Ibn 'Ali wa Abdullah Ibn Ja'far*, Number 2036, 4 folios. History of Hasan Ibn 'Ali (the son of Ali).
13. *Qissat Abi SaHma ma'a 'Umar Ibn al-Hattab*, Number 1774, 4 folios. History of the Beginnings of Islam.
14. *Qissat gazwat Haybar*, Number 1111, 18 folios. History of the Beginnings of Islam.
15. *Qissat Abi Yazid al-bistami ma'a al-qissin wa l'ruhban*, Number 297, 4 folios. Mystical Muslim and Christian Monks.

16. *Qissat Yusuf*, Number 105, 34 folios; Number 687, 9 folios; Number 1073, 27 folios. History of Joseph and the Pharaoh.
17. *Qisas al-Anbiya'*, Number 53, 39 folios. History of the Prophets (Confirmed by A Quranic Surah).
18. *Qisas al-Anbiya'wa 'aHwalihim wa kayfa huliqa al- 'insan*, Number 1996, 348 folios. History of the Prophets (Confirmed by a Surah from the Quran) and History of the Creation of Man.
19. *Qissat al'isra'*, Number 3291. The Ascension of the Prophet.
20. *Qissat al-imam 'Umar Ibn Al-Hattab*, Number 3755. History of the Caliph Umar.
21. *Qissat al-jumjuma ma 'a 'Isa*, Number 3638. History of the Crane, cf. Number 8.
22. *Qissat al-jamal*, Number 3265; Number 3402. History of the Camel (Miracles of the Prophet and the History of Ali).
23. *Qissat Satih Ibn Gassan*, Number 3725. The Beginnings of Islam.
24. *Qissat al-sabiyy al-ladi mata bi-sawqi al-Nabi*, Number 3660. The Boy Who Died From Love of the Prophet (The Beginnings of Islam).
25. *Qissat al-Migdad wa 'Ali Ibn Talib wa Mayyasa*, Number 3739. The Beginnings of Islam.
26. *Qissat mawlid al-Nabi*, Number 3756. The Birth of the Prophet.
27. *Qisas al-Anbiya'wa al-SaliHin wa-l-Awliya'*, Number 3655. History of the Saints and the Prophets.

Ahmad-Baba Catalogue

1. *Qissat 'ahl al-Suq*, Number 1180, 2 folios. History of 'ahl al-suq, Inhabitants of Qidal (Mali).
2. *Qissat Tawaddud al-jariya wa ma jara laha ma'a al-'lama'fi hadrati amir al-mu'minin* (Harun al-Rasid), Number 932, 20 folios. History of the Sympathetic Scholar, see Haidara Number 17.
3. *Qissat futuH Ifriqya*, Number 1181, 94 folios. The Conquest of Africa.
4. *Qissat AsHab al-kahf*, Number 2369, 9 folios. The Men of the Cave (Compare this text with Syrian versions).
5. *Qissat al-Mutawakkil ma'a al-imam al-Junayd ba'da qatlihi al-Hallaj lamma 'arada 'ulama'Bagdad qatlahu ba'da ttihamih bi zandaqa*, Number 2606, 3 folios. Anecdotes On the Abbassides.
6. *Qissat al-mi'raj*, Number 1806, 4 folios. Ascension of the Prophet.
7. *Qissat 'isq bayna Bisr Ibn Hujr wa Hind al-Juhaniyya*, Number 1602, 4 folios. History of Love.
8. *Qissat malikat Saba'Balqis*, Number 1991, 10 folios. The Queen of Saba.
9. *Qisas wa 'asatir bi-l-Hassaniya wa 'aglabuha 'ala alsinati al-Hayawanat*, Number 3751, 10 folios. History In Local Dialect, Involving Animals (Most Likely the Genre of Kalila or Dimna).
10. *Qissat Abi Hazim*, Number 6196, 7 folios.
11. *Qisas min al-asatir al-Hassaniya*, Number 6113, 6 folios. History in Local Dialect (see Number 9 above).

Images

All the photographs of manuscripts were taken by
Seydou Camara.

The Map of Africa (page 10) comes from the book *L'Afrique noire*
by Olivier Meynier, Flammarion, 1914.

p. 36: René Caillié / akg-images.
p. 40: Francois Guénet / akg-images.
p. 41: IAM / akg-images

Acknowledgements

Jemia and J.M. G. Le Clézio, Amin Maalouf,
Roukia Hamate Ba, Francois Vignaux,
Émilie Leroux, Ali Ould Sidi, Marie-Geneviève Guesdon,
Roland Colin, Abdel Kader Maig, Constant Hamès,
Hamady Boucoum, Lahcen Taouchknt,
Jean-Louis Triaud, Ousmane Halle, Julie Peghini,
Nicolas-Martin Granel, Salem Ould El Hadj,
Francoise Haeck, Alain Anselin, Aissatou Mbodj-Pouye,
Jamal Addin Baddou, Abderrahim Saguer,
Samuel Sidibe, Jean-Francois Colosimio,
Louis-Francois Larnaud

Isabelle Laffont, Laurent Laffont, Michèle Fraudreau,
Sylvain Collet, Renelle Setton, Florence Nocca.

Anne-Sophe Stefanini, my editor.

À Anne-Sophie Stefanini, mon éditrice.

الي هذا السرمد و منها الليالي قوله تعلى اذ جعلتم الـ

سهد وعلى نيلا يفرموا عند مالها وابو القاسم وهو

لمشهور والبلا قال ابو اعذ السمرا بن عبيد السكـ

Achevé d'imprimer en octobre 2012
par Graficas Estellas - Espagne.
N° d'éditeur : 01. Dépôt légal : octobre 2012.